BLUEPRINT
The Second Key Stage 2 Topics Book

Joy Palmer

Stanley Thornes (Publishers) Ltd

Do you receive *BLUEPRINTS NEWS*?

Blueprints is an expanding series of practical teacher's ideas books and photocopiable resources for use in primary schools. Books are available for separate infant and junior age ranges for every core and foundation subject, as well as for an ever widening range of other primary teaching needs. These include **Blueprints Primary English** books and **Blueprints Resource Banks**. **Blueprints** are carefully structured around the demands of National Curriculum in England and Wales, but are used successfully by schools and teachers in Scotland, Northern Ireland and elsewhere.

Blueprints provide :
- *Total curriculum coverage*
- *Hundreds of practical ideas*
- *Books specifically for the age range you teach*
- *Flexible resources for the whole school or for individual teachers*
- *Excellent photocopiable sheets - ideal for assessment and children's work profiles*
- *Supreme value*

Books may be bought by credit card over the telephone and information obtained on **(0242) 228485**. Alternatively, photocopy and return this **FREEPOST** form to receive **Blueprints News**, our regular update on all new and existing titles. You may also like to add the name of a friend who would be interested in being on the mailing list.

Please add my name to the **BLUEPRINTS NEWS** mailing list.

Mr/Mrs/Miss/Ms --

Home address ---

--Postcode ------------------------

School address ---

-- Postcode -----------------------

Please also send **BLUEPRINTS NEWS** to :

Mr/Mrs/Miss/Ms --

Address --

-- Postcode ------------------------

To: Marketing Services Dept., Stanley Thornes Ltd, FREEPOST (GR 782), Cheltenham, GL50 1BR

First published in 1994 by:
Stanley Thornes (Publishers) Ltd
Ellenborough House
Wellington Street
CHELTENHAM GL50 1YD
England

A catalogue record for this book is available from the British Library.
ISBN 0–7487–1710–2

Typeset by Tech-Set, Gateshead, Tyne & Wear
Printed in Great Britain at The Bath Press, Avon

CONTENTS

INTRODUCTION

Blueprints *The Second Key Stage 2 Topic Book* is a teacher resource book for 7–11 topic work. It consists of an extensive structured bank of ideas for eight topics and 56 copymaster sheets and is a companion volume to *Topics Key Stage 2*. The book is organised around the demands of National Curriculum, but may be used just as successfully by schools wishing to pursue general topics that are not necessarily focused on the National Curriculum. All the topics are cross-referenced to National Curriculum attainment targets to help with your curriculum planning. The aim of **Blueprints Topics** is to provide you with a structured resource which will enable you to meet the growing need for properly planned and focused topic work with clear learning objectives and coherent activities related to National Curriculum.

With this in mind you will find that each of the eight topics in this book provides the following resources:

- a topic web that maps out the topic across the curriculum and gives an indication of attainment targets covered;
- a list of basic concepts that the topic introduces;
- seven practical activity sheets for pupil use.

Topics for inclusion in this volume have been selected and organised so that each has a principal location in two or more subject areas of the National Curriculum. As a whole, the book is organised so that there is a good balance of topic locations across the core and foundation subjects of the curriculum together with the cross-curricular themes of Environmental Education and Health Education. In addition to its principal locations, each topic has coverage of several other subject areas. A summary of the principal and other areas covered within the topics is provided in the matrix on page v. This will serve as a useful aid to planning. It will help forward thinking and the selection of topics so that coverage of desired curriculum areas over a period of time is accomplished.

No attempt has been made to grade or bank topics into levels. Activities within each are wide-ranging. Some are very appropriate for pupils working at the lowest levels of Key Stage 2, whilst others will be a challenge to the most able. It is anticipated that individual teachers will select and adapt the materials to suit the needs of individual pupils and circumstances. All the topics have been developed with such flexibility in mind.

Whilst every attempt has been made to link the suggested activities for each topic with National Curriculum attainment targets, it should be pointed out that precision and specificity are not always possible. In a number of instances, notably relating to English and History ATs, activities cover all targets and therefore they are grouped at the end of the list of activities on the topic web. As it is hoped that teachers will interpret and extend many activities according to their individual circumstances, it is also highly likely that attainment targets will be covered other than those indicated.

Matrix to show principal location of Topics in subject areas of the National Curriculum, and other areas covered

Topic	Science	English Drama	Mathematics	Geography	History	Art	Music	PE	Design & Technology	Environmental Education	Health Education
Conservation	○	○		○					○	●	
Leisure		○	○	○	○		●	●			●
Flight	●	○	○	○	●	○			○		
Spiders	●	○		●		○		○			
Signs	○	●		●		○					○
Colour	●	○	○	○	○	●					○
Sound	●	○		○	○		●			○	○
Space	●	●	○		○	○			●	○	

Key:　● Principal location　　○ Other subject areas covered

CONSERVATION

Environmental Education

- Priorities for saving the planet
- Glossary of conservation terms
- Locations for identification of conservation issues
- Waste and recycling
- Kitchen conservation – saving energy
- Problems with the ozone layer
- Acid rain/global warming
- Water conservation – focus on the bathroom
- Environmental audit
- Garden habits of a lifetime
- Wildlife hazards
- Spotlight on the supermarket
- Pathway to green living

English

- The day the Earth spoke
- Stories of wildlife in danger
- 'Compost' word games
- 'Green' books
- The future of the planet
- The world's most dangerous animal
- Debates on controversial issues

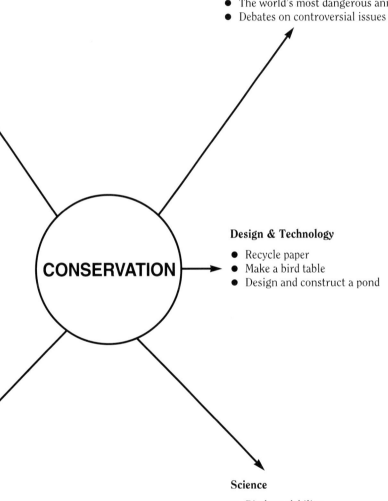

Design & Technology

- Recycle paper
- Make a bird table
- Design and construct a pond

Geography

- World issues – acting individually but thinking globally
- Conservation Club

Science

- Biodegradability
- Make a compost heap – rotting and decomposition

Note: Environmental Education is a cross-curricular theme of the National Curriculum. Thus by definition it crosses the boundaries of all other subject areas. The majority of activities included in this topic are therefore under the heading of Environmental Education, but many necessarily involve the skills and knowledge of other areas, notably Science, Geography, Art and English. A smaller number of activities which more closely fit the areas of Science, Design and Technology, English and Geography follow under these headings.

BASIC CONCEPTS

1 Conservation is a topic which affects the lives of all of us. Our homes and everyday surroundings are full of examples of how we might help to 'save our Earth'.

2 Whilst acting 'locally', we should also think globally. Conservation issues affect the whole world, and are no respecters of national boundaries.

STARTING POINTS

• Walk around the school building and its grounds. Make an 'environmental audit' – i.e. decide which positive and negative elements contribute towards your school's degree of environmental awareness. Signs to look for could include energy being wasted or saved, disposal of wastes, other form of pollution, etc.
• Watch a film or TV programme about aspects of

'Wildlife In Danger' – discuss the problems facing the diversity of life on our planet, and the need to take positive action to resolve these problems.
• Ask the children what they think the word 'conservation' means, and capitalise on their prior knowledge of issues, no doubt gained from the media, books, parents and previous school programmes.

ENVIRONMENTAL EDUCATION

Activity 1: What does conservation mean?
• Capitalise on the children's existing awareness of and concern for the environment. Ask them what they think the word conservation means: perhaps taking care of animals and plants in the world, perhaps protecting the countryside from damage, perhaps saving energy or taking bottles to the bottle bank …. Conduct a general discussion on the meaning of conservation and the need to take care of our planet Earth.

Allow children free rein for filling in **Copymaster 1.** After a class discussion, each child should be encouraged to decide on a priority for saving our world, and write a headline on the TV screen. They can surround the headline by an appropriate picture. Below the screen are the names of four TV channels. Let the

children decide on four priority areas for conservation, and write the titles of four imaginary TV programmes dealing with these areas by the side of the channels.

Extend this activity by letting the children write scripts for, or describe an outline content of, the programmes they have invented. **Note:** this activity may be undertaken more successfully after further knowledge and understanding of conservation have been acquired.
• Draw cartoon or realistic pictures of our planet, and annotate them with 'earth speeches' describing some of its conservation needs. This activity is designed to develop an understanding of the meaning of the term conservation through a sharing of ideas from members of the class.

Activity 2: Conservation – putting it into words

• Introduce key words associated with the term conservation. Write them on slips of paper and give one to each small group of children. Ask them to look these words up in a dictionary, consult reference books to find out more about the meaning, and report back to the rest of the class. Having discussed them and shared ideas, each group should write up their word as an entry for an illustrated glossary of conservation, which will be useful as a class reference book throughout the topic as a whole. Key words should include: resources, environment, pollution, waste, species, habitat, atmosphere, diversity, recycle, energy.

• Encourage children to understand that, while environmental problems are global, every individual can act 'locally' to help save the world. In order to develop this understanding, analyse the children's personal environments to locate specific areas in which conservation strategies may be practised. Make a list of these places, to include the following:

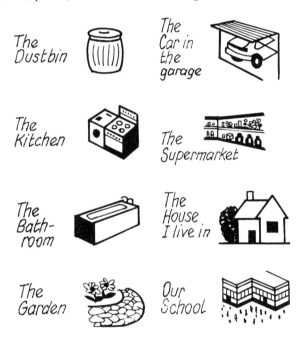

List the places to be considered

Record these places on a display accessible to the whole class. This display should merely record locations, symbolic illustrations and preliminary ideas. The following activities look at each of these locations in turn.

Activity 3: In the dustbin

• There's no better place to begin than in the dustbin! Ask children to explain to their parents about their topic work, and to investigate their waste bins at home. This need not mean rummaging through scraps – with cooperation from the family, a clipboard could be placed by the bin and everyone asked to record all items thrown away for a period of a week. Organise this so that the children divide up the sheet into categories of potential waste – these can be discussed and agreed in the classroom, so that results can be compared. For example:

What goes into the dustbin

This activity should reveal what an incredible amount and variety of rubbish an average family throws away. One British household disposes of around one tonne of waste each year. The category of 'others' should draw attention to larger items, perhaps made of more than one material – furniture, broken-down appliances and old toys – which have to be removed.

Activity 4: Recycling

• Discuss ways in which we can all help to conserve resources and materials, rather than simply throwing them away. Focus on the word 'recycling' and add it to your dictionary. Make 'recycling to save the world' posters:

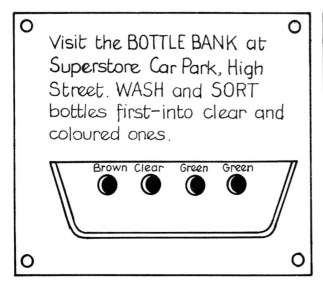

Visit the BOTTLE BANK at Superstore Car Park, High Street. WASH and SORT bottles first—into clear and coloured ones.

Brown Clear Green Green

Visit the SAVE A CAN SKIP at Bell Lane Community Centre WASH and FLATTEN cans.... Check to see if they are ALUMINIUM or STEEL

Aluminium   Steel
SAVE - A - CAN

• Find out the location of your nearest recycling centre. Visit places where it is possible to recycle plastics, metals, glass, paper. Take note of special instructions to be followed when recycling goods. Write details and instructions for others to learn, and display them around your school.

• Encourage recycling by making your own plastic, glass, bottle or can collecting boxes for school, or for the children to take home. All you need is some large cardboard boxes (preferably with purpose-made internal dividers for bottles) and paint or labels to decorate, with perhaps an instruction sheet for potential donors.

What to do:

1 Paint the outside of each box appropriately, or stick on labels from cans or bottles.

2 Stick on an instruction sheet to help people prepare their goods for your recycling box.

Collect plastic bottles for recycling

• Distinguish between magnetic and non-magnetic metal cans. Aluminium and steel ('tin') cans can both be recycled, but skips usually ask for separation. Use a magnet to test cans of various types–steel cans stick to the magnet, whilst aluminium ones do not.

• Make a class book of ideas for simple recycling strategies that do not involve trips to recycling centres. For example:

– pass on magazines and comics for someone else to read, perhaps a friend, doctor's waiting room or hospital

– pass on old clothes and toys to others who may like them, perhaps a charity shop or jumble sale

– save plastic shopping bags and use them again, instead of asking for new ones every time you shop

– keep plastic containers and use them to store things in, or turn them into plant pots!

• 'Recycle' plastic containers by using them to grow seeds in the classroom.

You will need:
old plastic containers, washed out (e.g. icecream and yoghurt pots)
a screwdriver
compost
seeds of cress and herbs

What to do:
Punch holes with the screwdriver in the bottom of each pot, to allow water to drain from the compost. (Children should be carefully supervised when carrying out this activity–or it should be undertaken by an adult.) Fill the pots with compost, sow seeds and label each container to indicate what has been sown. Keep the compost moist. If cress and herbs are grown, these can of course be eaten, and the teaching point made that money and resources can be saved if we grow our own food!

Re-use plastic containers

Activity 5: Conservation in the kitchen

● Ask the children to visit the kitchen at home and try to spot ways in which conservation can be practised. In particular, use this as an opportunity to develop the theme of energy conservation. Add the word 'energy' to your conservation dictionary, and discuss its various forms and their significance. Help children to appreciate that most of the energy we use in our homes is in the form of electricity, which is derived from fuels – usually coal, oil or gas. Some homes use gas for cooking and perhaps gas or oil for central heating. The key teaching point is that if energy in our homes is wasted, we are wasting valuable and limited supplies of the Earth's natural resources. Let the children make a list of kitchen appliances and note the form of energy which each of them uses. This activity could, of course, be started in school: if meals are prepared on the premises, then visit the school cook at a convenient time and ask him/her to explain what energy is used in the school kitchen.

● Make 'Kitchen Conservation' displays – perhaps a large kitchen scene collage could be created on the classroom wall, or separate posters made. Include pictures of appliances and work going on in the kitchen, with clearly written labels suggesting ways to conserve energy, for example:

Activity 6: How to be 'ozone friendly'

● Use discussion of refrigerators as a starting point to introduce the important topic of the damage being done to the ozone layer. Few children will associate global warming and 'greenhouse gases' with domestic refrigerators! Chemicals called chlorofluorocarbons (CFCs) are used in the cooling systems of fridges, and in aerosol sprays and certain types of foam packaging. These chemicals destroy ozone, which forms a protective layer between the damaging rays of the sun and the rest of the Earth's atmosphere (see activities in the topic 'Hot and cold' in **Blueprints** *Topics Key Stage 2*, pp. 8–9). Draw diagrams to show the position of the ozone layer, and add suggestions about how to be 'ozone friendly'.

5

Share car with other people. Take 1 car not 2!!

Take car to shops once a week not every day.

Change car to one that uses lead-free petrol.

Leave the car at home – walk or cycle!!

• Find out more about the 'environment unfriendly' nature of the cars we drive. Gases from exhaust fumes contribute to air pollution, making clouds slightly acid. When it rains, the rainwater can contain enough acid to pollute rivers, lakes and streams, and damage buildings. (**Note**: smoke from power stations and factories and waste fumes from buses, lorries, trains and planes all contribute to this problem of acid rain.) Let the children think of as many ways as possible of reducing damage from exhaust fumes. Record suggestions on a concertina-style book, with a car on each page and clouds above. Colour the clouds in increasingly lighter shades of grey as suggestions proceed.

• Test the acidity of the rainwater that falls in your area. Buy an acid rain testing kit from the WATCH organisation, a wildlife and environment club for young people.

Background information
The address of WATCH is 22 The Green, Nettleham, Lincoln, LN2 2NR. Members of WATCH receive a club magazine three times a year, containing lots of articles and practical suggestions for conservation. Why not write and find out about your local WATCH group?

• Help children to appreciate the link between these issues relating to the atmosphere. The so-called 'greenhouse gases', which act like a blanket and prevent some of the sun's heat returning to space, include CFCs, carbon dioxide, nitrous oxide and methane. As fossil fuels are burnt by industry and power stations, fumes are expelled by cars and CFCs are released, so the quantity of greenhouse gases increases. (**Note**: this can link to a study of tropical rain forests because, as the forests are burnt, so carbon dioxide is released into the atmosphere.) Draw a diagram to show the consequences of atmospheric pollution:

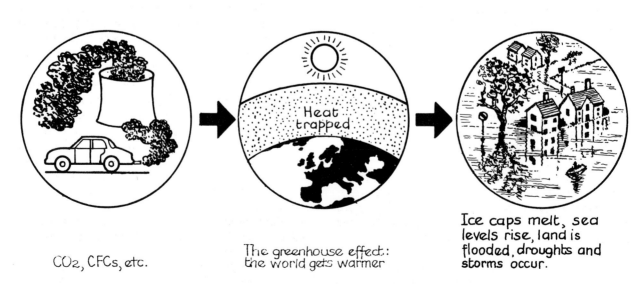

CO_2, CFCs, etc.

The greenhouse effect: the world gets warmer

Ice caps melt, sea levels rise, land is flooded, droughts and storms occur.

The consequences of atmospheric pollution

Activity 7: Conservation in the bathroom

● Turn attention from the kitchen to the bathroom as a location for conservation activities. Use this as an opportunity to introduce the key issue of water conservation. Children will no doubt enjoy making a toilet display!

Conservation in the bathroom

Activity 8: Audit your home

● Do a 'conservation audit' of your school building (link with Starting Points), and suggest that the children do the same for their own homes. Use **Copymaster 2** for children's personal recording of their home audit, and prepare a similar wall-sized poster for the school. Each child should consider various aspects of their home building (water tanks, roof, windows, walls, door) and colour the small square adjacent to its label on the picture. Colour the square green if the home feature is 'conservation friendly', and red if it is not. By doing a school audit first, you can come to agreement about what makes these features worthy of a green box. For example:
– if water tanks are lagged to save energy, colour green.
– if the roof is insulated, colour green.
– if windows are double-glazed or draught-proofed, colour green.
– if doors are draught-proofed, colour green.
– if heating is regularly serviced or gas/electric meters regularly monitored, colour green.
Don't forget to colour the house also!
● The second part of this audit can be done inside the home. Bearing in mind the key issues raised so far (including water conservation, ozone-friendly goods and recycling), let children colour a leaf on the tree beneath the house for every positive activity they can identify in their house. Ask them to write a sentence accounting for each green leaf, and explain their household's conservation activities to the rest of the class.

Activity 9: Conservation in the garden

● From the house and school building, turn attention to gardens and school grounds. Begin by taking a walk around the school grounds, drawing attention to specific sites and potential for conservation activities. Encourage the children to make suggestions for possible site development. **Copymaster 3** provides an outline recording sheet which can be used on either a home or school site. It gives a useful habitat checklist, and space to sketch or note enhancement activities. For example, a child could make an entry such as:

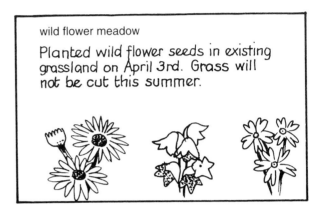

● Enhance all habitats to encourage animal, bird and insect life. This will necessarily mean having areas of untidy, long grass and attracting what tidy gardeners think of as weeds. Many insects adore nettles! If this is a school-based project, you will need to secure the support and enthusiasm of other people, including the Head Teacher and staff, the Governing Body and interested parents who will provide help and support in the development of the site (perhaps by digging a pond, planting trees or donating plant cuttings and seeds). Let the children draw plans of the existing school grounds and of their vision of future developments. Accompany these with written descriptions of specific projects and lists of items and help needed. Present these to the various parties concerned.
● Summarise potential developments for gardens or school grounds on a large wall frieze. This can be a whole class project. Individuals or small groups can contribute suggestions for conservation and make their own relevant section of the collage. The following activities may be included:

- Sow native wild flower seeds to make a meadow. Do not cut it until the summer *after* the flowers have grown and seeded.
- Leave some grass to grow long, a perfect home for insects and small animals.
- Plant a hedgerow, a home for birds to nest, insects and animals to live.
- Make a pond to attract water creatures.
- Make piles of logs and leaf litter. These will encourage minibeasts and hibernating animals such as hedgehogs.

- Plant some trees, preferably grouped, as a home and restaurant for insects, animals and birds.
- Plant flowers which will attract insects, especially butterflies.
- Grow plants on a wall – a home for insects and food for birds and animals.
- Add window boxes and plant containers, filled with flowers that will attract insects and birds.
- Grow some weeds in an 'out of sight' corner: stinging nettles are excellent food for the caterpillars of many beautiful butterflies.

A conservation area

Note: see also Science and Design and Technology activities. The key teaching point for all activities based on garden and school grounds development is, of course, conservation of wildlife and the need to protect the natural environment.

● Watch wildlife in the garden, school grounds and on class visits to woodland, countryside and urban areas. Provide food, water, shelter and nesting sites in appropriate places (see Design and Technology activities for a simple bird table design). Bird boxes, bat boxes, food containers and water baths are all simple and inexpensive to provide. Consult wildlife books and the RSPB for ideas on designs for bird boxes. Simple feeders can be made from milk cartons and water baths from upturned dustbin lids.

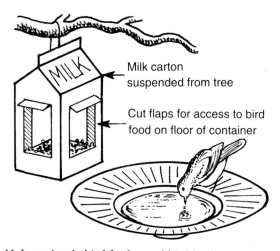

Milk carton suspended from tree

Cut flaps for access to bird food on floor of container

Make a simple bird feeder and bird bath

8

- Make a hedgehog shelter, and encourage hedgehogs into your garden by putting out scraps of bread and water. (They also like dog food.) Make a hollow in the ground, and place food nearby. Fill the hollow with a bed of dry autumn leaves. Cover it with logs or a wooden plank, leaving an entrance hole.

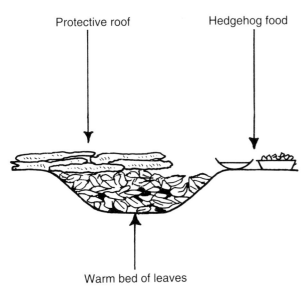

Protective roof   Hedgehog food

Warm bed of leaves

Make a hedgehog shelter

- Draw pictures to show 'Wildlife In A Wood', 'Wildlife In A Stream', 'Wildlife In A Town Street' and so on. Undertake more specific inventories of species seen and record numbers, names and dates: it is important to pursue this activity at different times of the year, so that seasonal changes, perhaps caused by hibernation and migration, can be noted.
- Make food chain pictures or mobiles to show links with feeding systems in various habitats, e.g. a woodland, a canal bank, an old churchyard. Draw arrows on pictures or link up mobiles in correct order to show 'who eats whom'.
- Remember that people too are part of food chains.

Ask the children to make a list of all the foods they eat in one day, and to draw food chains or webs to show how human beings fit into energy systems.
- Make large paintings or collages to depict hazards to wildlife and its conservation. Let the children design these and perhaps use them in a quiz, by asking other members of the class or school to spot the issues depicted. For example, they might include waste pouring out from a factory into a stream, dangerous litter left lying around, chemicals being sprayed on to land, trees being felled, etc.
- Take the class to visit a supermarket (organise this with the manager, and perhaps s/he will be willing to talk to the children about ways in which the store is aware of conservation and environmentally friendly practices). Ask children to note down observations of 'conservation at work' in the store. Display the results on a wall display entitled 'Shopping For The Earth'. Pictures and writing might illustrate, for example:

- organic produce on sale (grown with the aid of compost and natural manures, not chemicals)
- cosmetics/shampoos on sale that have not been tested on animals
- biodegradable or re-usable bags at the checkout
- biodegradable household cleaners advertised
- displays of kitchen paper and toilet rolls made from recycled paper.

- Summarise the above environmental activity by letting the children play the game drawn on **Copymaster 4**. Two children can play this game, but need their own Copymasters to colour. They will need a counter each and one dice. The players should take it in turns to shake the dice and move forward the appropriate number of squares from the start. Instructions must be obeyed when 'move forward' or 'move backward' squares are landed on. Children should colour − squares in red and + squares in green, to reinforce the message. As the game proceeds, they should draw sketches in the blank squares they land on to depict aspects of our world which we should conserve.

SCIENCE

Activity 10: Biodegradability
- Explore the concept of biodegradability, and add it to your dictionary of conservation terms. Take a series of six plastic containers or jars. Three-quarters fill them with moist soil from the school garden. Bury the following objects, one in each of the jars: leaf, coin, plastic spoon, piece of paper, apple core, piece of bread.

Cover the jars with clear film wrap, and leave for two weeks. At the end of this time, carefully tip the soil out of each jar and observe the objects. Note and sketch any changes. Replace the contents of each jar, and investigate again after another week. Repeat the process, and record results by sketching the objects at each stage of observation.

1 leaf 2 coin 3 plastic spoon 4 piece of paper 5 apple core 6 piece of bread

Results of Observations

Jar	14 days	21 days	28 days	35 days
1	*(leaf)*	*(partly rotted leaf)*	*(rotting)*	disappeared
2	○	○	○	○
3	*(spoon)*	*(spoon)*	*(spoon)*	*(spoon)*
4	*(paper)*	*(torn paper)*	*(fragments)*	disappeared
5	*(apple core)*	*(apple core)*	*(core)*	*(core)*
6	*(bread)*	disappeared		

Which things are biodegradable?

- Write about the significance of biodegradability for conservation issues, for example:

 – Leaves and 'natural' objects rot speedily away and help to make rich, fertile soil.
 – Plastics and other chemicals are not biodegradable. If thrown into soil or water they stay there and may pollute or poison it.

- Add a note about biodegradability to your kitchen and bathroom displays, for example:
 – Use biodegradable washing powders, sink and bath tub cleaners.
 – Read labels and buy environmentally friendly household supplies.

- Make a compost heap (link with environmental education activities, and with the topic on Gardens, **Blueprints** *Topics Key Stage 2*, pp. 59–68). Ask parents or school cook/garden maintenance staff to save vegetable food scraps and grass clippings. Build a compost bin by erecting square posts for corners and securing wire mesh around the outside. Fill with a layer

of soil, followed by a layer of manure if this can be obtained. Next, add a layer of your food scraps/lawn cuttings/weeds. These layers may be repeated. Cover the top layer of vegetable food scraps/lawn clippings with straw or a piece of old carpet and leave it to work! Discuss why wire mesh is used (compost likes oxygen) and why meat scraps should never be added (attract unwelcome rats!). After about six months, examine the contents of the bin and observe that the vegetable scraps/clippings have rotted to make compost, a form of good rich soil. Put the compost to good use!

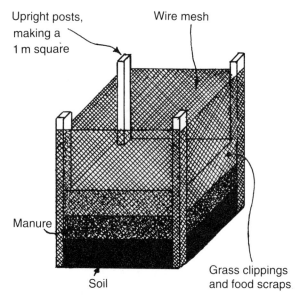

Upright posts, making a 1 m square   Wire mesh

Manure

Soil   Grass clippings and food scraps

A simple compost heap

- Link the above activity with the previous one on the concept of biodegradability. Things which rot to form compost are biodegradable, and are helped to break down by nature's decomposers (worms and bacteria in the soil). Use **Copymaster 5** to extend understanding of these concepts. Children should place the two particular food items (i.e. a slice of bread and an apple core) in a clear plastic bag, make small holes in the bag and place it near the top of the compost heap – on the food scraps, under the carpet cover so that it is easily found. Observe the bag and its contents every three days. Each child can sketch his/her observations in the rectangles on the Copymaster. Almost certainly, children will see the foods shrivelling up and rotting away, perhaps growing mould, and no doubt 'attacked' by worms, insects and other creatures of the soil. Explain the crucial role of fungi, bacteria, worms and insects in breaking down organic waste. (See also the topic on Rocks and soil in **Blueprints** *Topics Key Stage 2*, pp. 25–6.)

DESIGN AND TECHNOLOGY

C6

Activity 11: Making recycled paper
- Make some recycled paper.

You will need:
some used paper

warm water
two wooden frames of the same size
some fine wire netting or plastic mesh
a large water container.

What to do:
Cover one of the frames with the fine netting.
Prepare paper by tearing it up and soaking it in warm water overnight. Mash it up with your hands or a vegetable masher.

Place frame A on top of frame B. Dip them vertically into the pulp, then sweep them through the pulp and lift them out horizontally, so that the surface of the netting is spread with a thin layer of pulp. Allow water to drain off. Remove frame A. Turn the layer of paper pulp on to a flat surface covered with an old tea towel or kitchen cloth. Cover with another cloth, then layers of newspapers. Press down hard. Uncover and leave to dry.

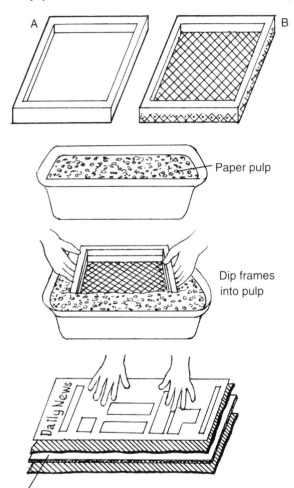

Paper pulp

Dip frames into pulp

Layer of pulp between cloths and covered with newspaper

Making recycled paper

Activity 12: A DIY bird table and pond
● Make a bird table with the aid of **Copymaster 6,** which shows how a very simple design can be modified for two locations. Take a simple wooden plank or tray. Either drill holes in its four corners and thread plastic-covered, waterproof clothes line through these holes and hang from a tree branch, or secure the plank or tray to an upright post and 'plant' it in a suitable place.

Background information
Birds are shy and prefer tables in sheltered places, perhaps near trees, though this encourages the arrival of squirrels who you may not wish to eat all your bird food! It is possible to squirrel-proof a bird table by securing an upturned dustbin lid two-thirds of the way up its supporting post. Remember to do some research on the kinds of foods that various species of birds like – put out something for them all. It is better not to feed birds in summer when natural food is plentiful; peanuts especially can be dangerous for young nestlings in the nesting season.

● Design and make a simple pond for home or school (involve parents for help with digging if this is to be anything other than a very small project). Bear in mind that, in order to be a successful wildlife habitat, the water needs to be at least 1 m deep, and safety precautions will be needed at all times when it is complete. First, design the pond on paper, then draw out its shape on the ground. Dig out the hole, so that the deepest part is in the centre and the sides rise in a series of steps. Line the hole with a sheet of PVC plastic, sold for the purpose. Place a layer of soil some 15 cm deep in the bottom. Secure the PVC sheet with bricks at the edge while the pond is filled with water. Preferably fill it from an existing pond, so that tiny creatures will be transferred. They will soon multiply and attract others. If possible, obtain small plants from ponds belonging to people you know, or buy water plants from a garden centre. Don't fill the pond right to the top – leave space for rain! If this is to be a true wildlife pond, do not add goldfish. They will eat the eggs and tadpoles of frogs, toads and newts.

Dig out the pond, with `steps' of different depths

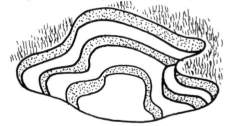

Line the pond with heavy-duty polythene

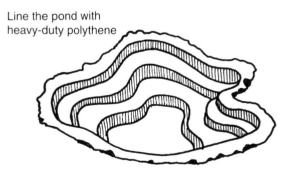

Fill the pond with pond water

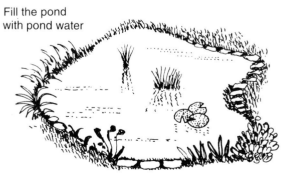

A simple pond will attract more wildlife

ENGLISH

Activity 13: Saving the world
- Write accounts of 'The Day The Earth Spoke' – compose imaginary 'Please save me' speeches that might have been delivered in the recent past by our long-suffering planet. Let the Earth deliver its own cry for help, explaining what needs to be done to save it, why and how.
- Write imaginary stories about wildlife in danger of losing its natural habitat; for example, thoughts of a fox as it witnesses the removal of its woodland home, the cries of frogs as their pond dries up, the conversations of voles and mice as their hedgerow habitat is replaced by a wooden fence, etc.

Activity 14: Compost vocabulary
- Use **Copymaster 7** to help children understand the basic ingredients of good compost. These words can be added to your conservation dictionary. At the top of the page are words to be unjumbled. Below is a word puzzle with hidden 'compost' words which can be found by reading horizontally or vertically. Mark these words when found by drawing a box around them.

Answers
Jumbled words: micro-organisms, organic material, soil, moisture, oxygen.
Hidden words: decompose, moisture, micro-organism, rotted, soil, oxygen.

Activity 15: 'Green' stories
- Read some of the very many 'green' children's stories now published. Consult the *Green Book Guide* published by Books For Keeps (1990) for guidance on choice, or talk to your local librarian.

Activity 16: Look into the future
- Discuss and write imaginary scenarios for the future of our world. The children's vivid imaginations should conjure up images of doom, gloom and hopefully optimism too. Use this activity as an opportunity to introduce debate on issues not mentioned elsewhere in this topic, notably nuclear power and renewable energy sources.
- Write stories entitled 'The Most Dangerous Animal In The World' – a description once applied to human beings. Ask children to explain the significance of this accusation.
- Organise class debates on the 'pros and cons' of various topics associated with conservation issues. For example, debate:

'Air travel' – a wonder of the modern world?
'Pre-packaged Foods' – help or hindrance?
'Motorways' – the answer to our travel needs?
'Rain forests' – source of world timber?

GEOGRAPHY

Activity 17: Global thinking
- Whilst acting locally, children should be encouraged to think globally – all the issues highlighted under Environmental Education activities can be considered on a global scale. Do this by linking the topic with a study of distant lands, as required by the National Curriculum for Geography. Select countries beyond the UK which have suitable case studies of issues such as tropical rain forest destruction, water pollution, acid rain, nuclear energy, soil erosion and destruction of good farming land. Study these as specific international examples and relate back to reference points in the children's own lives. The key teaching point is that conservation is not a localised issue. The world needs a global agenda for conservation if our planet is to be saved. Let the children explain in writing the need for 'individual action but international co-operation'.

Activity 18: Conservation club
- Organise a class 'Campaign For Conservation' or Conservation Club. Make advertising posters, membership cards and badges, and draw up some rules of membership (ideally involving personal action!). Children in schools with desktop publishing facilities could use these to design membership cards and posters, and even produce regular newsletters. The campaign/club should be publicised to raise awareness of activities that the children are undertaking. Hold regular club meetings and perhaps invite outside speakers to come and talk about their interests in conservation, how it affects their work and so on. Above all, emphasise the importance of each person acting locally in order to make a worthwhile contribution to the cause of conservation.

Save Planet Earth

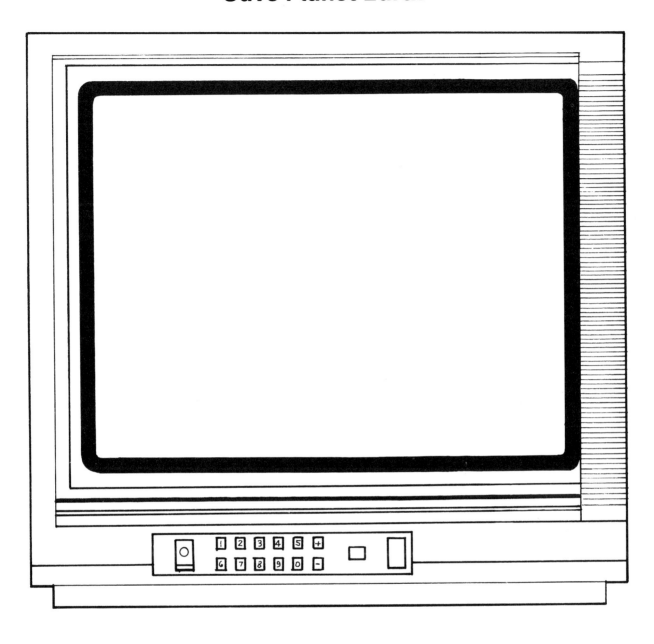

Channel 1 _____

Channel 2 _____

Channel 3 _____

Channel 4 _____

Audit your home

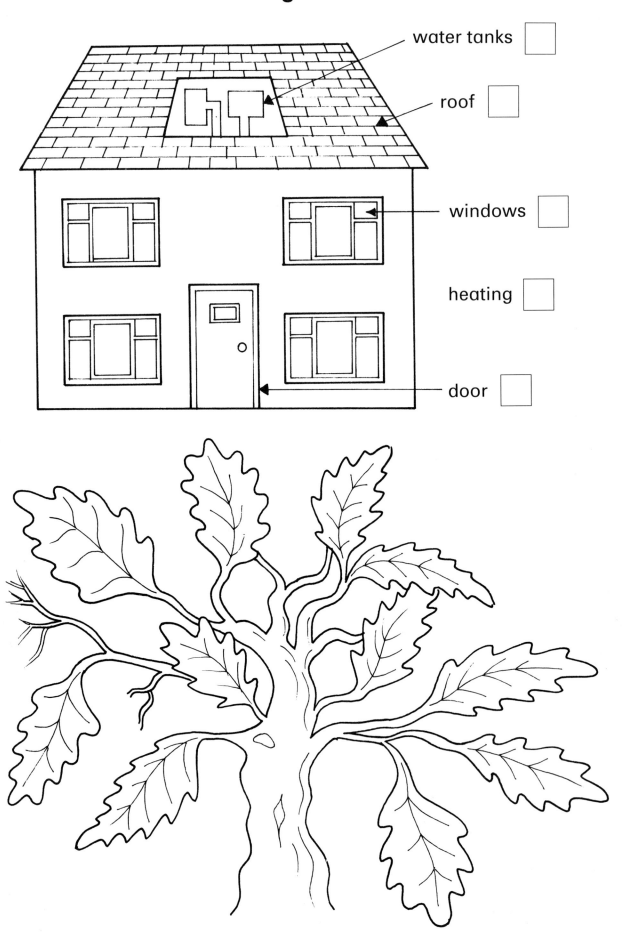

water tanks ☐

roof ☐

windows ☐

heating ☐

door ☐

Habitat action

wildflower meadow	long grass
hedgerow	wall
window boxes/containers	trees
flower garden	leaf litter/logs
pond	bird/bat boxes

Pathway to green living

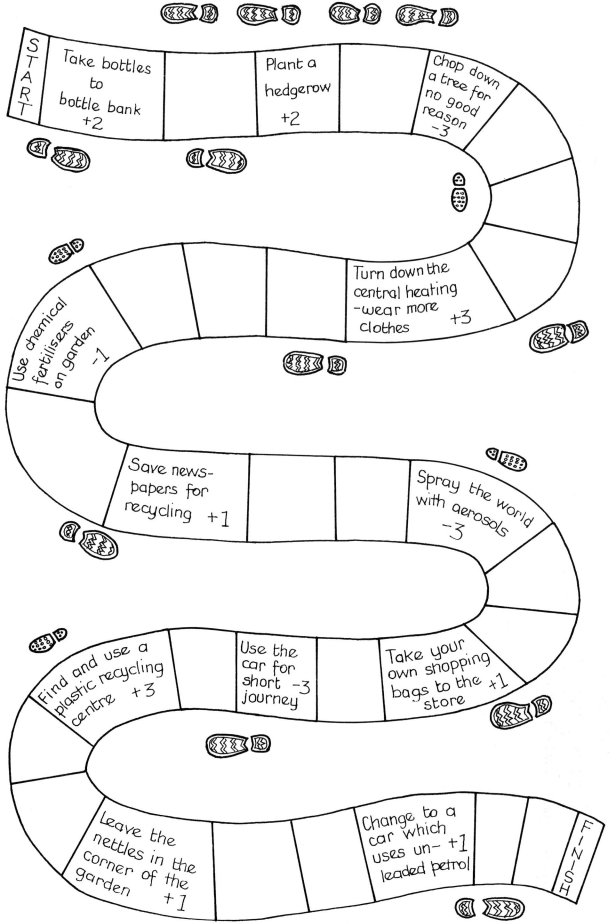

START

Take bottles to bottle bank +2

Plant a hedgerow +2

Chop down a tree for no good reason -3

Turn down the central heating -wear more clothes +3

Use chemical fertilisers on garden -1

Save news-papers for recycling +1

Spray the world with aerosols -3

Find and use a plastic recycling centre +3

Use the car for short journey -3

Take your own shopping bags to the store +1

Leave the nettles in the corner of the garden +1

Change to a car which uses un-leaded petrol +1

FINISH

Rotting away

0 days	3 days

6 days	9 days

12 days	15 days

Making a bird table

Unjumble the words to find things that make good compost:

1. crimo gnrosamsi   _____

2. rcinoag aeamrlti   _____

3. oisl   _____

4. osmirute   _____

5. ynoegx   _____

			D	A	F	H				
		O	X	Y	G	E	N			
		Q	B	N	P	P	O			
	C	K	Y	Z	S	G	A	O		
	D	E	E	R	T	C	N	B		
L	D	E	C	O	M	P	O	S	E	
R	X	Y	Q	T	O	M	P	M	A	
I	J	R	W	T	I	V	K	Z	L	
E	W	X	V	T	E	S	J	I	J	K	Q
D	C	L	A	X	D	T	I	B	O	S	H
V	Y	M	I	U	U	U	T	U	P	O	G
M	M	I	C	R	O	O	R	G	A	N	I	S	M
G	F	S	F	Z	W	H	E	F	V	N	L	R	S

LEISURE

History

- Leisure in ancient times
- Greek and Roman games
- Origins of the Olympic Games
- Medieval sports and pastimes
- Leisure in Tudor and Stuart times
- Leisure in Victorian times
- Origins of modern sports
- Leisure 'then and now'
- Invent a new game or pastime
- Present-day leisure needs

PE

- Sports for pleasure – classifications
- Choosing a sport
- Sports for 'free'
- Sports festivals/games
- Pleasure or profit?
- A sporting career
- Aerobic/anaerobic exercise
- Playground games
- Indoor games

Mathematics

- Board and counter games
- Numbers for fun

Geography

- Leisure in distant lands
- USA television
- Holidays and travel
- Leisure as an industry
- Be a tour guide
- Environmental impact of leisure

Health Education

- Leisure time survey
- Need for exercise and rest
- Energy for leisure/calories and food
- Metabolic rates
- Benefits of exercise
- Stress and relaxation
- Abuse of leisure – smoking, alcohol, drugs

Music

- Favourite songs and music
- Musical styles for relaxation
- Desert Island choices
- Accessing music for pleasure

English

- Reading and writing for pleasure
- Literary visits
- Crosswords and word puzzles
- Leisure place poetry
- Stories of sportsmanship
- Value of television

Note: This topic is also included as a named aspect of local history which could be studied as a Supplementary Study Unit of the National Curriculum for History, i.e. it is an aspect of the local community to be studied over a long period of time.

BASIC CONCEPTS

1 Our leisure is the time we have when we are not working. Everyone needs a certain amount of leisure.

2 Many things can occupy our leisure. Some activities need us to be active, and others to rest. We need a balanced combination of both of these.

3 Leisure pursuits have changed over the years since the days of the world's first people. Present-day society has continually growing needs for the provision of leisure time activities.

STARTING POINTS

• Find out how the children in your class like to spend their own leisure time. Conduct a survey, and make a distinction between very active and passive pursuits.

• Make a collection of pictures of sports and games that can occupy our leisure time. Include both indoor and outdoor activities.

• Talk about what facilities are available in your local community for occupying leisure hours.

HEALTH EDUCATION

C1–3

Activity 1: What do you think?
• Ask the children to define the word 'leisure'. Suggest that they write down what they think it means, then read out their definitions. As a whole, the class will no doubt have differing views. To some, leisure may be a term conjured up by the gym apparatus and swimming pool of the so-called 'leisure centre' in the community. To others, it may be a funfair, an idea derived from their knowledge of 'leisure parks', whilst some may consider leisure time to involve lounging around and doing nothing. Discuss the fact that indeed all these answers are correct – leisure is the time we have when we are not occupied with work or other things we have to do. A wide variety of activities can occupy our leisure time.

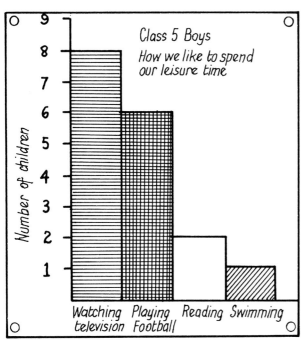

• Conduct a class survey to find out how members of the class like to spend their own free time. Ask them what their favourite leisure-time occupation is, and plot ranked results on a graph. After drawing a complete class graph, divide the responses into those of boys and girls, rank them again and draw new graphs to highlight any gender differences.

Activity 2: Work, rest and play ...
• Show children **Copymaster 1** and use this first as a basis for a class discussion on what are good and not so good ways of spending one's leisure time. No doubt some children will think the top picture represents an ideal way of spending spare time, whilst others will far prefer the lower one! Conclude the discussion by helping children to appreciate that both these activities, i.e. exercise and rest, are very important if we are to keep our bodies healthy. Let children colour the pictures, then write sentences beneath them explaining the importance of exercise and rest. This activity can then be extended by looking more closely at the need for both of these things.

• Relate the importance of exercise and rest to the concept of energy. Both these things require energy, and if we do not take care of our bodies and help them get the energy they need, then we will not be able to fully enjoy our leisure. The key teaching point is that it takes energy to make things move, and the more we move, the more energy we need and use.

• **Copymaster 2** will help the children to appreciate these fundamental ideas. First, let them read and colour the sheet, thus making the mental link between food intake and energy output. The bottom sentence should be completed, introducing the key word 'calories'. Explain how our bodies get energy by 'burning up' the food we eat in our muscles (see also Hot and cold in

Blueprints *Topics Key Stage 2*, pp. 3–4), and that we measure the amount of food energy we take in, and the amount burned up, in units called calories.

Activity 3: Calorie charts

● Consult specialist books (on weight watching, exercise and diet) to investigate the calorific value of common foods. Many food wrappings now contain this information. Make a chart of 'Calories We Eat' and display it on the classroom wall. Use this as reference material for various calculations – each child can calculate roughly the number of calories eaten during a particular meal, or in a day. Ask the children to calculate the calorific value of the foods depicted on **Copymaster 2**. Point out that this is not such a simple task as it might appear – for example, a burger meal may contain mayonnaise, ketchup, cheese, mustard and fat for frying, as well as the obvious bread and burger!

● Research the number of calories burnt up per minute in various activities, and make a parallel chart. Remember to include sedentary occupations – these require energy too! Let children work out how many calories are burnt up by the activities shown on **Copymaster 2**, if each is performed for 10 minutes. There is again scope for extensive mathematics work – children can calculate their own calorific expenditure during specific activities, or over a day.

Background information
To be technically correct, energy is measured in very small units called joules (J). A thousand joules make up 1 kilojoule (kJ). Food wrappings often show the number of kJ that a type of food contains, and the equivalent number of kilocalories. The 'calorie' with which we are more familiar in everyday parlance is actually a kilocalorie (1000 calories), often written as Calorie to distinguish it from the calorie.

● Discuss what is considered to be an appropriate number of Calories for one individual to consume in a day. This could perhaps lead into a sub-topic on food and the energy efficiency of various meals.

Background information
Most adults need just over 2000 kilocalories a day to keep healthy, whilst growing children need slightly more.

Activity 4: We need exercise – and rest

● Discuss what happens if too few or too many calories are consumed. (**Note:** this is an issue to be approached with sensitivity, as children or their relatives may have a 'weight problem'.) The significance of this in the context of the present topic is to make children aware that if all our leisure time was spent sleeping, we would probably become very overweight individuals.

● With older children, introduce the concept of metabolic rate. They may well challenge the above theory and claim to know very thin individuals who take no exercise and eat lots, or overweight people who

hardly ever seem to eat. Let them know that metabolic rate, or the rate at which chemical reactions occur inside an organism, varies widely from person to person. Circumstances also affect the rate – when people are under stress or exercise regularly, the metabolic rate is increased. People with high metabolic rates can eat large amounts without putting on weight because breakdown of food happens so fast that not much fat is stored. People with low metabolic rates put on weight easily and usually have little energy.

● Make posters to display other reasons why exercise is good for us, as well as for speeding up our metabolism and helping us not to get fat. Display these around the school where parents and visitors can see them, as advertisements for using our leisure time wisely.

Activity 5: We need our sleep

● Return to **Copymaster 1**, and remind children that rest is also very important for our bodies. Liken the body to a battery: if it does not get recharged, it will 'wind down' and not function properly. Point out that children need more sleep than adults, because they have growing to do! Ask children how many hours sleep (on average) they have each night – bearing in mind that, rather like metabolic rate, individuals vary greatly in their needs.

● With the children, make a list of reasons why we need sleep, including:

- Lack of sleep makes us feel tired or ill.
- Lack of sleep affects our concentration.
- Sleep helps our muscles to relax and stay healthy.
- When asleep, our bodies 'repair themselves', i.e. growth hormones help body tissues to grow.

● Make annotated displays to show the link between stress and relaxation.

Full of anxiety, the body produces hormones to gear it into action. The result is tension and feeling tired. Constant stress gives us headaches and makes us ill, perhaps seriously ill.

The cure for stress is to relax. Calm down, relax muscles, breathe deeply. Forget work – have some fun!

● Find out more about and illustrate ways in which some people find relaxation.

Emphasise the importance of being able to relax and the fact that our leisure time should be spent in a combination of active and passive pursuits.

Activity 6: Health hazards

● Introduce the 'three great evils' of leisure with **Copymaster 3**. Explain that, unfortunately, some people use methods to help them relax which are very bad for them – especially smoking, alcohol and drugs. Let children colour and consider the three evils, as depicted on the left-hand side of the page. On the right hand side are boxes for writing about the reasons why these leisure pursuits are definitely to be avoided.

Elaborate upon this activity by delving into each of the problems in greater depth and letting the children paint posters warning others of their dangers. Perhaps the class could be split into three groups, each investigating one problem and then sharing results. The final products could be a dramatic wall display of posters entitled 'Leisure Can Kill', and a class assembly educating others about the temptations of smoking, health and drugs. It may also be possible to invite a visitor from the local health authority to talk to the class and answer their questions.

● Make a collection of advertisements for cigarettes and alcohol. Study them carefully and discuss the power of print, and the temptation to try whatever product is being promoted. Note that health warnings about the dangers of smoking are often in very tiny print compared to the glossy pictures and promotion messages. Note also that alcohol advertisements do not tell us how many 'empty' calories adults are consuming with each glass of liquid (i.e. calories that do not supply a useful source of food energy). Take large sheets of poster paper and divide them in two: on one half display advertisements for cigarettes and alcohol, cut from magazines and newspapers, and on the other half paint pictures and slogans which counter and contradict the advertisements.

Meditation   Massage   Quiet pursuits

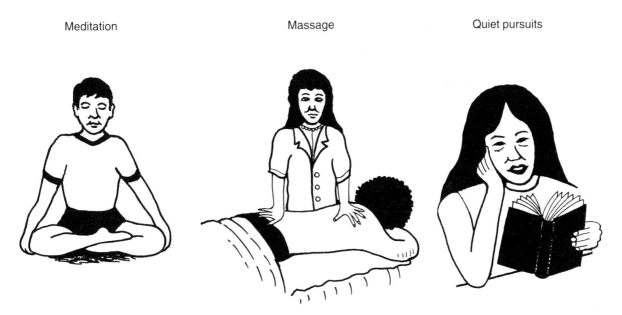

Some quiet ways of relaxing

● Draw an outline of a human body, labelled to reinforce the evils of misuse of leisure.

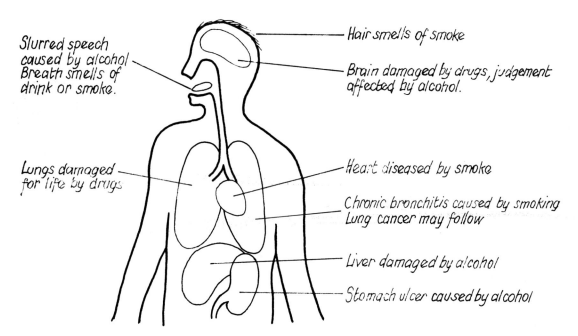

Slurred speech caused by alcohol. Breath smells of drink or smoke.

Hair smells of smoke

Brain damaged by drugs, judgement affected by alcohol.

Lungs damaged for life by drugs

Heart diseased by smoke

Chronic bronchitis caused by smoking Lung cancer may follow

Liver damaged by alcohol

Stomach ulcer caused by alcohol

Would you like this person to be you?

PHYSICAL EDUCATION

C4

Activity 7: Sporting endeavours

● Make a large collection from magazines, comics and travel brochures of pictures of people taking part in a variety of sports and games. Ask each child to make his/her own individual collection, and then to contribute to the class collection. Study these and sort them into sets to show the range and variety of leisure-time games. Let children suggest sets – for example, water sports/sports for land; team games/individual games; active sports/passive pursuits; indoor games/outdoor games; those which need specialised equipment/those which do not; those which require specific skills/those which do not ... the possibilities for classification are numerous.

Activity 8: Check it out
● One of the benefits of this activity is that it encourages children to find out about sports with which they are not familiar, and encourages participation. Use **Copymaster 4** as a basis for discussing one particular category of leisure sports, i.e. those that require water. Let children identify the sports, using reference materials if necessary, and colour the pictures. They can read more about these sports and, if possible, talk to someone who does them, thus discovering what specific skills and equipment are required. This activity helps children to appreciate that:

– some sports need specialist equipment and locations
– many sports require particular physical skills
– skills need to be practised regularly
– some sports are more expensive than others to pursue.

● Let each child adopt one active sport and conduct an in-depth investigation of it, referring to points mentioned in the previous activity. They should produce an illustrated book about their sport which provides information that others may wish to know – including how to go about learning the sport, what equipment, if any, is required, and why the sport is particularly good exercise. Tell the children that the purpose of their book is to promote their sport amongst those who know nothing of it. It should be a comprehensive advertisement for why we should spend our leisure time doing it. Let each child make a poster to depict their sport. Display books and posters next to each other as a 'Sport Library', which all children and visitors to the classroom can consult.
● If you have a leisure centre or sports club in the local community, ask the manager if s/he would be willing to come and talk to the class about its facilities, telling them something of the benefits of taking part in the activities provided. They should bear in mind age restrictions that may apply to children. It may even be possible for someone connected with a particular local sporting club (e.g. cricket, athletics, football or rugby) to visit the school to explain their sport, demonstrate some of the skills or even hold a coaching session for interested participants. Alternatively, can the class arrange to visit the club?

Activity 9: Sporting tournaments
● Children will no doubt take great interest in 'exotic' sports, perhaps expensive ones or those difficult to pursue in the average neighbourhood, such as scuba diving, paragliding, American football, etc. Help them to understand that a wide range of 'free' exercise is available to us all. Let them make a list of sports and exercise that involve little in the way of equipment (walking, jogging, skipping, jumping) and write promotional notes, telling others of the benefits of these.
● Do a sub-topic on a festival or major event which involves active sports, such as the Olympic Games or the Commonwealth Games – investigate the various sports which make up the event, and find out about the routines of the athletes. Discuss the personal qualities

of 'good sportsmanship', as well as the skills needed. Explain to the children the words which are the basis of the Olympic spirit, as dictated by Pierre de Coubertin when he organised the first modern games in 1896:

'The most important thing in the Olympic Games is not to win but to take part, just as the most important thing in life is not to have conquered but to have fought well.'

This activity will lead to a consideration of professional and amateur sports status, the significance in this context being a differentiation between 'leisure for pleasure' and 'leisure for profit', or 'play for pay'.
● Ask the children to discuss whether they think this pleasure/pay distinction exists. Pose the question of whether they would like to be employed full-time in a sport they love and at which they are very successful. This activity would be an excellent starting point for imaginary stories describing their sporting prowess! Let them think beyond the immediate attraction of this, to realise the pressures involved and the commitment to fans, audiences, the public and press. Organise a class debate on the justice of professional sports people being paid huge sums of money for doing what they enjoy. Display points on either side of this debate, so that others may consider them:

A SPORTING LIFE

● I have lots of money.
● I enjoy winning, and most of the time I do.
● I love seeing my picture in the newspapers
● People pay me to advertise their products.
● I have power.... and GLORY!!

● I get lots of letters begging for money
● If I lose, the press give me a really hard time.
● People expect me to win every match I play in.
● If I feel tired, it's hard to take time off.
● Soon I shall be too old to be so successful. Younger people will take my place.

Activity 10: Respiration
● Distinguish between aerobic and anaerobic respiration (link to activities on energy and the importance of exercise in the Health Education section). Draw diagrams to show the position of our lungs, or breathing organs, with annotations to explain their function:

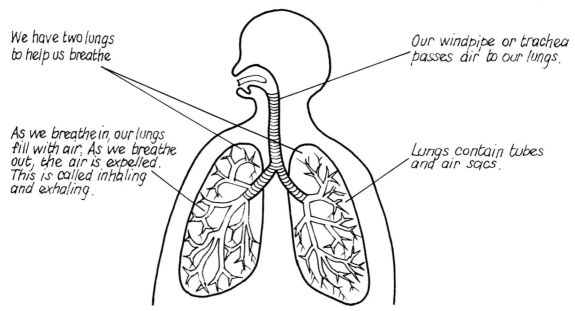

We have two lungs to help us breathe

Our windpipe or trachea passes air to our lungs.

As we breathe in, our lungs fill with air. As we breathe out, the air is expelled. This is called inhaling and exhaling.

Lungs contain tubes and air sacs.

How we breathe

● Write a series of sentences on worksheets for children to fill in gaps with missing words relating to respiration, for example:

Gases enter and leave our ☐

Tubes carry ☐ into our lungs.

These are surrounded by air sacs and blood ☐

Aerobic respiration needs ☐ which is brought into our cells by our ☐

Fill in the missing words

The answers are: lungs, air, vessels, oxygen, blood.

Use this activity to help children make the link between physical exercise, breathing and oxygen, and to appreciate that aerobic exercise is very good for us all, unless done to excess.

Activity 11: Playground games
● Play some games in the playground which offer good aerobic exercise, but which are not common sports as such. For example:
– play chain tag. One player is 'it', and has to run around and catch someone else. When caught, the second person links hands with the first, and the two run together to catch a third … and so on. The last

person to be caught by the chain is the winner. (You could split the chain once it has six people in it.)
– play 'Shipwreck'. Place some 'islands' (e.g. mats, tyres, hoops, paper or anything that can be landed on) around the playground. One child who is 'on' chases the others, who are safe when they land on an island. Make sure that the children know that they cannot stay on their island beyond a count of 10. Once caught, a captive takes the place of his/her captor, and the game begins again. Alternatively, the captives can then help the original chaser to catch the rest of the children, with the last survivor starting the next game as chaser.
– organise aerobic races, including three-legged, running backwards, skipping, obstacle, kangaroo (children have a large rubber ball between their knees) and sack races.

There are numerous books of indoor and outdoor games available nowadays with plenty of other suggestions.

Activity 12: Indoor games compendium
● Make a class book of well known (or perhaps not so well known!) indoor games, with children writing and illustrating all the instructions. Whilst these may not offer good aerobic exercise, they are valuable leisure pursuits to be played for relaxation or exercising the brain! Let each child contribute at least one game to the book, and ask parents or friends for suggestions too. If well written and illustrated, this activity could result in a publication worthy of a wider audience – make copies to sell to parents at the school Open Day, summer fayre or Christmas bazaar. Schools with access to desktop publishing facilities would find this a most worthwhile project to embark upon. Suggestions for contents include card games, art and craft activities, pencil and paper quizzes, marbles, board games, treasure hunts, puzzles, indoor races and other competitions.

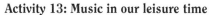

MUSIC

Activity 13: Music in our leisure time
● Investigate the tremendous role that music making plays in our leisure time. Conduct surveys to find out the titles of the children's favourite songs and pieces of instrumental music. Graph the results. This activity could, of course, be extended throughout the school, in order to find the 'Top of the Pops' or 'Top Twenty' at the end of a particular week, month or year.

Activity 14: Do you play requests?
● Schools with the technology could perhaps make a tape-recorded programme of requests from the children to be played over the classroom P/A system or issued on cassette to individual classes. Groups of children could be involved in selecting the music to be played, writing the links between records, announcing the items and recording the programme. It might also be possible to arrange a visit to a local radio station, in order to see the professionals at work.

Activity 15: Dear listener …
● Listen to music of various kinds in the classroom, including pop, jazz, classical, old-time dance, country and western, and popular songs from various decades. Listen for enjoyment, and listen to them critically. Seek the children's ideas about musical styles. Let them consider what sorts of music would enhance their leisure and which would cause more stress than relaxation!
● Play a version of 'Desert Island Discs' – ask each child to list, with reasons, the eight pieces of music they would take to accompany them on a desert island. Share decisions with the class as a whole. Adult colleagues

may agree to let the children hear *their* choice of music and memories, too.

Activity 16: Music all around us
● Talk about the various ways in which we can access music in our leisure time, including buying records, cassette tapes, compact discs and music videos, as well as listening to radio, watching television and going to concerts. Find out about concert halls, orchestras, amateur productions and other possibilities for musical entertainment in your local community. Make a booklet giving details of the location of these places, and how to get tickets. Include prices and sample programmes if available.
● If a suitable musical production or concert programme is available, arrange a class visit to a matinée or evening performance. Such an activity should include preparing the children for the performance by familiarising them with both music and story, as well as making them aware of conventional behaviour on such theatrical occasions. Productions such as 'Oliver!' and 'Joseph And His Amazing Technicolour Dreamcoat' are ideal for older children to attend, containing as they do plenty of colour, action and melody.
    It is sometimes possible to arrange a visit to the theatre when the manager or one of the staff is prepared to show the children round the backstage area. If this can be arranged immediately prior to attending the evening performance, the children can find this particularly interesting – especially if they manage to catch a glimpse of some of the performers! Wherever possible, the entertainment profession gives very generously of its time in this regard, and may well respond positively to requests from schools.

MATHEMATICS

C5–6

Activity 17: Fun with numbers
● Children may not readily appreciate the association between mathematics and leisure! Help them have fun with numbers, and introduce them to a range of activities which require an application of mathematics – including many card, board and counter games, as well as mathematical puzzles and challenges. Begin with the simple challenge provided on **Copymaster 5**. This can be done at any stage when the children have some free time – thus representing what leisure is all about, choosing an activity for enjoyment. The task is to count the number of small and large circles on the page. The best clue to success is to suggest that the children colour them as they go along, so that they can see what has already been counted. [There are 13 large circles and 44 small circles.]

Activity 18: Maths monster
● Another fun activity, requiring a little more

mathematical skill, can be found on **Copymaster 6**. Children can play this in pairs, but need their own Copymaster to colour. Provide two dice and a shaker for each pair of children. Numbers must be thrown in sequential order to complete a monster, starting with a 1 for its body. Each player should start by using only one of the dice until the number 6 is reached, and thereafter they will need to throw both dice in order to obtain an aggregate 7 or 8. Remind the children that they will need to throw two 3s, two 4s, two 6s and two 7s. The 7s and 8s can be made up in any combination of numbers. Players should colour in their monster as they go along. The winner is the first person to shake an 8, colour the mouth and correctly add the total at the bottom of the sheet.

● Much mathematical activity can be generated by a class mini-athletics meeting, in terms of timing the races, measuring distances and recording the results.

ENGLISH

Activity 19: A 'Good read'
- Develop an appreciation of writing and reading as enjoyable leisure pursuits. Encourage the children to tell others about their favourite story or author. Make a display of the results, thus suggesting a 'good read' for others.

Activity 20: A book fair
- Try to develop a close link with the library, and organise a book fair over a period of, say, one week. Enlist the help of the local librarian to arrange book displays. Some paperback publishers may provide children's books on a sale or return basis, and it may be possible to hire a travelling exhibition. See that your selection of books is displayed as attractively as possible. Encourage the children to contribute illustrations and book reviews of their own. Every effort should be made to arrange for experts in the field, such as a writer of children's stories, an illustrator, a publisher, a bookseller or a librarian to visit the school and talk about their work with books.
- The children might work together to produce their own book, either a single story or an anthology, with groups taking responsibility for one or more aspects of the enterprise – from the writing of the stories, the illustrations, the desktop publishing (if the school has the technology), assembling the finished product, and the marketing/sales activities.

Activity 21: Literary visits
- Arrange a class visit to houses or museums in the local community which are connected with great writers. It may also be possible to visit other sources of literature, such as local newspaper or magazine offices, in order to learn more about how these publications are produced.

Activity 22: Word games and puzzles
- Make up crossword puzzles and other word games for children to solve as spare-time activities. Produce a class book of word puzzles, with contributions from children and their parents.

Activity 23: Poetry
- Read the works of some well known poets, such as William Wordsworth, who wrote of the beauty of places where they spent their leisure time.

Activity 24: Write it yourself
- Write stories called 'The Good Sport' and 'The Bad Sport', telling of people who demonstrated great sportsmanship – or lack of it.

Activity 25: Television
- So far, no mention has been made of television, one of the most popular forms of leisure entertainment – sometimes known as the 'goggle box' or 'the haunted fish tank'. Do any of the children perhaps have an odd family nickname for the TV set? If so, collect and illustrate them for a display. Organise a class debate on 'Television – a mixed blessing'.
- Discuss the value of various types of television programme in terms of helping people to relax and enjoy their leisure time. Conduct a survey amongst teachers, parents and children to find out their views on 'the most entertaining television programme'.
- Ask the children to schedule a night, or perhaps a week, of balanced television entertainment which they think will have something for everyone. Results could be recorded in a TV magazine style format, especially if schools have access to desktop publishing facilities.
- Some families may have access to cable or satellite television. Ask the children to write about how these services are broadcast.
- Perhaps children could invent a cable or satellite company of their own. Ask them to choose a name and design a logo and posters to advertise this new company, and write about what programmes can be seen on the new channel. A number of these contributions would make an eye-catching display.
- Ask the children to discuss television advertising – which are their favourite commercials, and why? Do they believe all the claims of these advertising campaigns? Perhaps older children could attempt to analyse some of the advertising techniques involved in selling these products to the public. Create advertising posters, slogans, jingles, etc., for imaginary new products and display them inside large cut-out television screens on the classroom wall.

Write your own advertisements

These new products might include:
- a better mousetrap
- a new burglar alarm
- a device to wake lazy children in the morning
- something to put children to bed at night
- a squirrel-proof bird feeder
- a delicious new drink
- a new labour-saving household appliance
- a snack with a new flavour
- a new, environmentally friendly form of transport
- a new brand of washing powder,
and so on.

GEOGRAPHY

Activity 26: Leisure around the world

• Find out as much as you can about leisure in different parts of the world, perhaps linking this with a study of a distant land to cover a programme of study for the National Curriculum for Geography. Great contrasts will be found, for example, between how Inuit families amuse themselves and how native rain forest tribes spend their time. Make a large display on 'World Leisure' showing interesting sports and pastimes associated with faraway lands.

• **Copymaster 7** provides a splendid opportunity for discussion on how even something as commonplace as television varies considerably around the world. This schedule shows programmes available on a Thursday evening in Los Altos, California–without taking account of cable programmes, of which there are many. Even without these, the viewer has a choice of 20 channels. Let children spend time reading and considering this, then prepare a series of questions for them to answer on a separate sheet, for example:

1 How many movies can you choose from?
2 How many channels show the news?
3 Which programmes appear on more than one channel?
4 Which programmes are also shown in Britain?
5 Are any British-made programmes shown in California?
6 Name various sports you could watch.
7 How many programmes are in languages other than English?

Activity 27: Holidays and travel

• For many people, leisure means holidays. Visit the travel agent and collect a number of brochures for the class to browse through. Ask each child to plan 'My dream trip', and describe with the aid of maps and illustrations where they would go, given no restrictions on time and money.

• Investigate the leisure 'industry' in this country, and consider why we use this term. Make a class list of job possibilities associated with helping people to enjoy their leisure. These should include hotel manager, waiter/waitress, tour operator, coach driver, courier or tour guide, leisure centre attendant, gardener, bingo hall owner, funfair proprietor … the list is almost endless. Write job descriptions for a selected number of 'leisure time personnel', perhaps those chosen by children as jobs they would like to do.

• Let children imagine they are tour guides for foreign visitors coming to their own locality. (This can be done anywhere!) Plan a route to incorporate highlights of the neighbourhood, and write the guide's speech. This may well help the children to appreciate buildings or facilities in their neighbourhood which are generally taken for granted.

• If the locality is not particularly conducive to this idea, ask the children to suggest the ideal leisure facilities they would like to see in the area, and describe them in both words and pictures.

• Design pictures/posters warning of the dangers or problems for the environment associated with tourism, for example:

Don't remove rocks; our valuable Earth is being worn away by people.

Enjoy your picnic, but take your litter home!!

Some of the problems caused by leisure activities

HISTORY

Activity 28: Leisure time, then and now
- What do the children think is the oldest toy in the world? Why? If they could find one of these toys, what would it look like?
- What is the oldest game in the world? How do the children think it might have been invented?

Both these questions should lead to some interesting speculations. Can the class find evidence to support their theory?

- Ask the children to imagine themselves as having been born in another age. What would they have looked like? What toys might they have played with? How were these toys made? What other skills would they have been learning? If they had been born in another time, which one would they choose, and why?

The children should make this a subject for a piece of creative writing, prior to undertaking some historical research as to whether their chosen period would really have lived up to their expectations.

Let the children draw pictures of themselves as, for example:

- a prehistoric
- an ancient Egyptian
- an ancient Greek
- an ancient Roman
- an Anglo-Saxon
- a Viking
- a Norman
- a medieval
- a Tudor or Stuart

boy or girl, and so on.

This activity would be ideal for group work, provided the class has access to adequate resource material on clothing of the chosen period. For added 'authenticity', the children could provide a small portrait photograph of themselves (preferably full face). Each group could concentrate on drawing the head (cutting out a hole for the face) and body, clothing it appropriately and then cutting it out. Pictures could, of course, be drawn, painted or created in collage materials. The photograph could then be placed behind the figure to make the whole thing realistic, and displayed on a suitable period background.

The groups should then conduct some detailed research on what life might have been like for children in their chosen period of time, recording their findings in pictures and writing. Can they find historical (i.e. archaeological) evidence such as vase paintings to support their investigations? Afterwards, with the benefit of research behind them, the children could write a second piece summarising their findings.

- Provide a suitable background sheet on which to record findings about childhood during the various different periods of history – roles, activities, toys and games played, other leisure pursuits and so on. Alternatively, provide a quiz sheet like this one, on which children may record their suppositions and findings:

PERIOD OF HISTORY: _____

GIRLS   BOYS

ROLES: What things did they learn? Why?

ACTIVITIES: How did they spend their spare time?

TOYS: What toys did they have to play with?

GAMES: What games did they play? (Draw some of them)

Background information
The children should discover a number of differences between the ways in which the young were educated long ago, compared to the systems in use today. One imagines that the further back in history one travels, the more important was education for survival. In many civilisations, the division between rich and poor, slave and freeman, is there for all to see, whilst the role of women has been subservient to that of men throughout the centuries (and many would say that there is still a considerable way to go before true equality is attained – if ever!). The oldest toys may have been model animals: baked clay horses abut 2500 years old have been found in Egypt.

- A study of the origins of the Olympic Games would provide much information about the sports and pastimes of the early Greek civilisation. What were the sports events originally included in the Olympic Games? How many new competitions have been included nowadays? The children could write imaginary accounts of their participation in such events, and there is plenty of scope for art work of all kinds.

Background information
A number of games, sports and pastimes played in those early days in Greece can still be found today. They include arm wrestling, leapfrog, spinning tops, knucklebones (sometimes known as jacks or fivestones), dice games, tug of war, skipping, bowling hoops, variations on 'tag' chasing games, marbles, blind man's buff, numerous ball games and piggyback fighting. A messy and fairly pointless game known as 'kottabos' was often played at the end of a party, when

young men would take a little wine in their cups and try to hit a given target in the room. There is also a vase painting showing two warriors playing some kind of board game, and a carving which seems to depict a game of hockey.

• Ask the children to play as many of these games as possible – consistent with their own safety, of course.
• Make a study of games and pastimes in Tudor times for both children and adults. Emphasise the fact that children in poorer families continued to learn skills of farming and the like in order to ensure their survival – few ever learned to read or write. The children of rich families, on the other hand, were much better educated, and could afford to indulge in more recreational occupations. Highlight the contribution of Henry VIII and his court to the country pursuits of hawking and hunting for deer, hares, wild boar or foxes. Ask the children to find out what a 'bear garden' was.
• Debate the rights and wrongs of these 'blood sports'.
• Ask the children to write a diary entry, a sort of 'Day In The Life' of a rich child and one for a poor child living in Tudor times. What contrasts and activities can they find to write about?

Background information
The Tudor age saw a number of cruel sports taking place which would not be allowed nowadays, including bear baiting and cock fighting.

• Create a collage or wall display, showing Tudor and/or Stuart pastimes.
• Can the children find out what the game of 'bandy-bar' was? Perhaps they could draw a picture of what they think the game looked like. A clue: the name may refer to the unusual shape of a piece of wood used to play the game.
• Which King of England wrote a 'Book of Sports' in which he listed acceptable games which could be played after attending church on Sundays?

Background information
Children continued to play traditional games such as leapfrog, hide and seek and hopscotch. Bowls appears to have been one of Drake's favourite games. 'Bandy-bar' was a game similar to golf. The royal sporting writer was James I.

• The children could find out about the Puritan attitude to games and pastimes.
• In Stuart times, the theatre was a popular place of entertainment. The class could undertake a sub-topic on the history of the theatre and produce a good deal of creative writing and artwork. Ask the children to find out:
– when did performances take place? Why?
– how were sound and stage effects made in those days?
– who played the parts of women in these plays?
– why did fashionable ladies in the audience often wear elaborate masks?

Perhaps they could make a model of Shakespeare's Globe Theatre.

• What was Charles II's 'sporting' nickname? Which games did he like to play?
• How was the game of 'pell-mell' played?

Background information
Charles II, nicknamed the 'merry monarch', enjoyed yachting, hunting and playing tennis. He was also fond of the theatre, and attended horse race meetings at Windsor and Newmarket. New sports at this time included angling and cricket, whilst 'futeball' had few rules and little restriction on numbers in a team: indeed, whole villages are known to have taken part, using the streets of the neighbourhood as a pitch, and at one time the game was banned because of the injuries and damage it caused! At this time, the royal parks such as Hyde Park were first opened up for public use by Charles II.

Indoor pastimes included chess and draughts, as well as cribbage, dominoes, billiards, and dice and card games. Making music, dancing and attending masques were popular with wealthy families.

• Another fruitful period to study is that of Victorian times. Contrast, once again, the lives of rich and poor children and compare them with childhood nowadays. How did children amuse themselves in those days?
• Ask the children to discuss this extract from the writings of Douglas Jerrold (circa 1850), concerning a nine-year-old girl who was sent to work in a factory:

'It is five o'clock on a January morning. The child is up, and with its scanty covering pulled about it, descends slowly to the street. (After nine hours at work, the girl returns home to) … seek oblivion from the noise, the racking noise of engines, the hell of sounds which she has all day suffered … A very, very few years pass over her head, and at sixteen, at most, she is probably a wife …'

Little leisure time for her, one suspects!
A flower girl once remarked of her family, 'Mother pawns the blankets, and father beats mother and swears awful. We ain't got no Sunday things; we're all raggety, so the Lord don't take much notice on us.'
Both these accounts give scope for creative writing and would make an arresting caption to art work of various kinds.
• Find out about the effect of these conditions on the health of working children. How did men like Lord Shaftesbury try to help these poor children?
• Contrast this with the life led by a well-to-do Victorian family, whose children were in the care of a nanny, had their own nursery and perhaps a governess to teach them the three 'Rs'. Their toys would include lead soldiers, china dolls, toy theatres, magic lanterns and peepshows, and quite often a beautiful rocking horse. Poorer children had to make do with rag dolls and simple, often home-made, toys like the whip and top, the hoop and stick or the cup and ball.
• If possible, visit a museum of childhood such as Sudbury Hall, near Derby, and allow the children to see the many magnificent exhibits there. They range from opulent dolls' houses, expensive dolls, toy soldiers, railway trains and teddy bears to all kinds of books,

Victorian childhood – rich and poor

board games and the ubiquitous Noah's Ark. Sudbury Hall also provides a Teachers' Pack containing a wealth of information and ideas for activities.

● The children could try to make some Victorian toys for themselves. The Sudbury Hall Museum resource materials contain instructions on how to make a whizzer, a thaumatrope, a kite, costume dolls and a toy theatre, amongst other items. Some craft shops nowadays sell reproductions of simple toys such as the cup and ball, and it may be possible for the children to try these games for themselves.

Ask the children to find out where the phrase 'penny plain and twopence coloured' originated.

Older children might like to make a rag doll or peg doll from scraps of material, or even attempt to embroider a sampler (a popular occupation for girls in Victorian times). Boys might care to make their own toy soldiers.

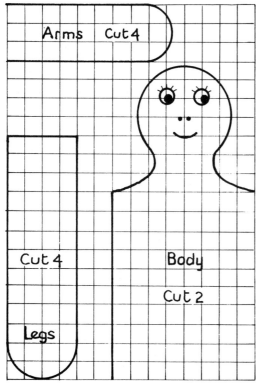

Make a rag doll or toy soldier

• The Pollocks Toy Museum and shop in London (1 Scala Street, London, W1) still supplies authentic toy theatres which children can assemble, and scripts such as 'Aladdin' and 'Jack The Giant Killer' which they can use. Perhaps a group of children could write and perform their own production to entertain the rest of the class.

• The class could paint or collage a large wall display depicting some of the many street entertainers who could be seen in Victorian times – including organ grinders, clockwork dancing dolls, conjurors, clowns, strong men, jugglers, sword swallowers, Punch and Judy, singers, stilt walkers and clowns.

Background information
Much detailed information on the street life of London can be gleaned from the contemporary books by Henry Mayhew (*Mayhew's London* and *Mayhew's Characters*). He describes many characters such as Michael the 'Italy man' and his dancing bear Jenny, with his assistant playing the pipes and drums, and Salamander, the fire eater. Apparently, Salamander swallowed fire for a small fee plus liquid refreshment 'for his mouth gets very hot!'; when he made a mistake, his moustache 'fizzed up'.

• Ask the children to find out what a 'penny gaff' was.

Background information
Penny gaffs were temporary theatres, often converted from old shop premises, where 'rude [i.e. rough and ready] pictures of the performers are arranged outside to give the front a gaudy and attractive look, and at night time coloured lamps and transparencies are displayed to draw an audience … on a Monday night as many as six performances will take place, each one having its two hundred visitors'. This kind of entertainment was much enjoyed by the lower classes of Victorian times, consisting as it did of vulgar comedians, singers and, in the words of one small child 'flash dancing, they show their legs and all – prime!'

• Another institution worthy of investigation would be the Victorian music hall. The children could learn some of the famous music hall songs or hear some well known monologues. Many of these have been preserved on tapes, records and in books, including the adventures of 'Albert and the Lion' and 'Sam's Musket' (recorded by Stanley Holloway). Contemporary artistes like Roy Hudd and the duo Cosmotheka have a great interest in preserving this material, and it may be possible to hear their work too. Both the penny gaff and the music hall offer scope for imaginative writing and all kinds of art work.

Background information
Music halls flourished in the 1880s and 1890s, with famous artistes like Marie Lloyd, Dan Leno, Albert Chevalier, Little Tich, Gus Elen and many more. Some halls gave as many as four shows a night, with programmes boasting singers, dancers, acrobats, trick cyclists, comedians and other entertainers.

In 1892 Albert Chevalier (singer of 'My Old Dutch' and 'Knocked 'em in the Old Kent Road') wrote an account of his life as a London music hall performer which included the following:

'I do four halls every night, and on Saturdays two matinées as well. I begin each night at the Royal in Holborn at about 8.30; about 9.30 I go from there to the Canterbury in Westminster Bridge Road; at 10.30 I am at the Tivoli in the Strand; at 11 o'clock I am due at the Pavilion in Piccadilly Circus. As a rule I sing three songs at each, though I try to get off with two. I used to sing all my songs in one rig-out with the exception of 'The Old Kent Road', and then had only to don a different coat and waistcoat. But now, for 'My Old Dutch', I have to make a change from top to toe, paint and the rest of it, but I can do the whole change in two minutes, and have in fact done it in less. Then back to my original dress – a change I can do in one minute – for my last song, and I am in the right costume also for my first song at the next show. Sometimes I have had to get out of my brougham [carriage] on my arrival at the next hall, and walk straight from it onto the stage.'

It may be interesting for the children to realise that a good music hall act could support many performers for much of their working life, since there was no radio or television to swallow up their material. When Chevalier sang 'My Old Dutch' in four music halls a night, it would have taken him four years to reach the same audience as might have watched him once on a television programme.

• Using Chevalier's account, the children could write imaginative stories about life as a music hall artiste. What might have happened had they been running late one evening?

• How many well known children's books from the Victorian period and beyond can the children find?

Which famous children's story does this extract refer to? It was written in 1905 by a schoolboy living in the slums of a big city:

'The story that our teacher was reading to us that afternoon … sounded lovely to me and I believed it all. I know where Mr and Mrs Darling live too. And Wendy. They live on Portswood Avenue in one of those big houses. Every day you can see the Nannies taking children for walks. I asked our teacher what a nursery was and everybody laughed – especially when she asked me where I played with my toys. I haven't got any toys except an old top which I play with sometimes under the bed. I don't suppose Wendy would ever look at a boy like me if she knew what sort of house I lived in. I felt very sad that afternoon as I walked home to our court (what a funny name to give to a collection of dirty houses). I knew Mother would be looking for things to pawn again, and I should have to take them round to the shop. Ever since the bailiffs had taken our furniture we had practically nothing except a broken table and a double bedstead.'

There is a considerable amount of social history in this extract for the children to explore, if time permits. Perhaps they could write about the sad slum boy, and what happened to him when he grew up.

• Another increasingly popular leisure activity with

THEN – when Victoria ruled our land . . . . . .

NOW – approaching the 21st. century . . . . . .

The seaside, then and now

the coming of the railways was the Sunday excursion to the beach or the countryside. The children could research and write about these 'day trips', as well as investigating the origins of new forms of travel such as the bicycle and the motor car which played an increasingly important part in the leisure activities of many families. Let the children hear or learn songs like 'Daisy, Daisy' or 'Get Out And Get Under', which make an incidental comment on the social history of the period.

• Draw pictures of 'Leisure time – then and now', such as the seaside scenes above.

Ask the children to write an account of significant changes in what they see (the nature of the beach games, clothing, sea activities, etc.) Similar pairs of pictures could be designed (by teacher or children) for other aspects of leisure, such as a sports field, countryside walk, visit to a railway station, and so on. Try to depict as many changes of lifestyle and leisure pursuit as possible within each picture.

• Further group work could take the form of investigations into the origins of our major sporting activities – sports such as fishing, cycling, tennis, football, cricket and rugby. Groups should produce an illustrated report and feed back to the rest of the class.

• Leisure time during this century has been revolutionised by the electronic age and modern technology – groups could explore the origins of recorded sound ('the wireless'), films, television, records, cassettes, compact discs, computers, video games and so on. If possible, show some of the classic silent film comedies of the Keystone Cops, Chaplin or Laurel and Hardy; let the children hear some of the old Children's Hour radio broadcasts too. A wind-up gramophone and some old 78 records would be of great interest, especially as a centrepiece to any classroom museum display. Remember to return any exhibits in good condition, together with a letter of thanks from the class.

• Bring the study of leisure pursuits up to date by conducting a survey amongst the children's parents, relatives, neighbours and friends. Ask the class to compile a suitable questionnaire which can be photocopied and used to collect information about the games and pastimes their parents and grandparents used to play. If the instructions are clear, children may be able to try some of these games for themselves. Perhaps the children can invite older people into school to tell them about 'the good old days'. The results of such a survey will make very interesting reading, especially if any old photographs or toys can be brought to school – perhaps for inclusion in a classroom 'Museum Of Leisure'. Schools with desktop publishing facilities could produce a fascinating document or book of childhood memories which would be of value and interest to future generations.

Twentieth century leisure

● Can the children learn anything about the children of long ago from the nature of the toys and games many of them played with? Would today's youngsters be satisfied with such playthings?

● See if the children can find out whether the pastimes of their parents ever got them into mischief, and if so, how? Record and illustrate any anecdotes as vividly as possible, perhaps in a booklet entitled 'Here's Another Fine Mess ...' or 'Nothing But Trouble ...'. If necessary, change the names to protect the guilty!

● Things commonly collected by children in the fifties and sixties included stamps, records, autographs, foreign coins, cigarette cards and so on. See if the children can borrow any of these items from family and friends to put on display in the classroom museum.

● An interesting sub-topic to consider would be a study of comics, past and present. Make a collection of as many different comics as possible – how many can the class produce altogether? What is the oldest issue they can find? How much did it cost? Of course, parents may well be able to help with names of their old favourites, even if original copies cannot be found, and some towns have 'nostalgia' shops where old children's comic annuals can be purchased.

Conduct a readership survey, (a) within the class, and/or (b) within the school, using duplicated question sheets. Collate the information on block or line graphs. Which is/are the most widely read comics? The answers received could be analysed under such headings as:

– Which comics are the most popular?
– Do more boys than girls read comics or vice versa?
– Which comics do younger children read?
– In each year of the school, which comics are read most?
– How many children buy comics?
– How much is spent on average by children each week?

Within the class, discover what the favourite comics are and display the result as a pie chart.

Create a wall display showing the most popular characters in children's comics nowadays. Record the results of this survey in an appropriate way, too.

Each child could take a bundle of comics and compile individual comparative lists, which would involve listing the price, size, number of pages, use of colour, content, etc., of each comic, together with a brief evaluation at the end. Questions to be asked could include the following:

– Is the comic funny?
– Is it a comic for girls, for boys or for both?
– What features does it contain?
– Which are the best items in the comic?
– Is it good value for money?
– Which are the most interesting characters in the comic?

The children could attempt to draw a comic strip of their own to develop a simple story line, say within a set number of pictures. This activity is not as simple as the children might think. Perhaps they could develop a new contemporary comic character.

● The same survey activity could, of course, be carried out during a study of old children's annuals.

Activity 29: Leisure in the future
● Discuss and write about the ever-changing needs of our present-day society in terms of leisure provision. With increasing unemployment, and many people working shorter hours, there is a growing demand for sport and entertainment facilities in Britain. Find out and illustrate examples of how this need is being met, for example, by the provision of community centres, leisure areas attached to shopping complexes, multi-screen cinemas, and neighbourhood sports pro-grammes. If possible, arrange a visit or interview people employed in the management of such facilities about their work and future plans for the leisure industry.

Good for your health

Energy to move

Everything we eat and drink provides our bodies with energy.

The more we move, the more energy we need.

We take in and burn up energy in amounts which can be measured.

These amounts are called

Bad for your health

SMOKING

Smoking relaxes me

cigarettes
cigars

ALCOHOL

I just love the taste of this

beer ... wines ... spirits

DRUGS

This makes me feel really good

glue ... LSD ... marijuana ...
heroin ... cocaine

Water sports

Write the name of each sport in the box underneath its picture.

Around and around

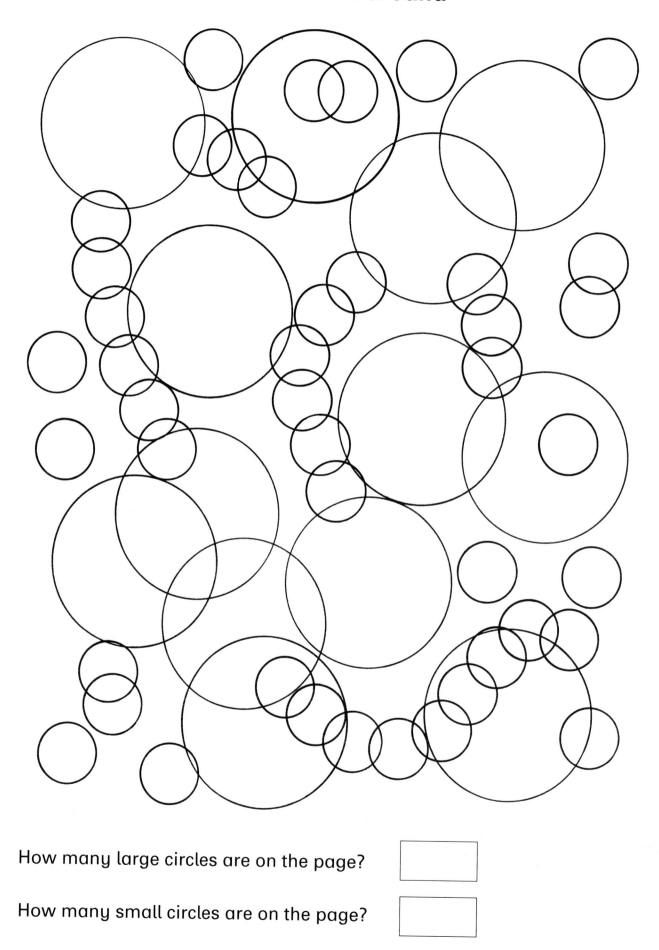

How many large circles are on the page?

How many small circles are on the page?

Maths monster

You must throw

1 for the body   5 for the tail

2 for the head   6 for each antenna

3 for each hand   7 for each eye

4 for each leg   8 for the mouth.

How many does he add up to altogether?

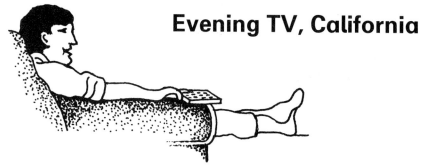

Evening TV, California

Channel	6.00	6.30	7.00	7.30	8.00	8.30
2	Boss?	Mama's	Cheers	Love Boat	The Simpsons	Drexell
4	◄——— News ———►		Wheel Of Fortune	Jeopardy	The Cosby Show	Different World
5	◄——————— Basketball ———————►					A Current Affair
7	◄——— News ———►		ABC News	Entertainment	◄——— Entertainers Top 20 ———►	
8	◄——— News ———►		Wheel	Jeopardy	The Cosby Show	Different World
9	◄——— News Hour ———►		Business Report	Q.E.D.	◄——— Skating ———►	
11	News	Hard Copy	First Edition	A Current Affair	◄——— Entertainers Top 20 ———►	
14	◄——— Noticiero ———►		◄——— Muchachitas ———►		Al Fiho	Fama
20	◄——— Hunter ———►		◄——— Perry Mason ———►		◄——— Gunsmoke ———►	
26	Meadows	Vietnam	Mandarin	◄——— Chinese TV ———►		
32	Que Pasa	Japan	Cooking	People	◄——— Beirut ———►	
35	Love Boat	Studs	Different World	Full House	The Simpsons	Drexell
36	◄——— Matlock ———►		◄——————— NFL Hockey ———————►			
44	Full House		◄——— Star Trek ———►		◄——— Movie ———►	
46	News	The Cosby Show	Married	Entertainment	◄——— Top Cops ———►	
48	Noticiero	C.N.N.	◄——— Manuela ———►		◄——— Los Años Perdidos ———►	
50	M*A*S*H	Cheers	News	Golden Girls	◄——— Nova ———►	
54	Pet Pourri	Wild America	Dr Who	Emmerdale	◄——— Movie ———►	
60	Japan	Cooking	◄——————— American Masters Golf ———————►			
65	◄——— The 7.00 Club ———►		◄——————— Praise The Lord ———————►			

FLIGHT

Science/Technology

- Things that fly – natural and machines
- Parts of a plane
- Forces of flight
- Power for flight
- Concepts of aerofoil
- The importance of flight
- Use of helicopters
- 'Lighter-than-air' craft
- Wind power – kites, gliders
- Hot air/hydrogen balloons
- Bird flight patterns
- Feathers for flight
- Why birds fly
- Natural flight
- Flight simulator

History

- Earliest attempts at flight
- Famous pioneers of flight
- The Wright Brothers
- The mystery of Amelia Earhart
- A flight timeline
- Military aircraft – World Wars I and II
- Famous air battles
- Military plane insignia
- History of passenger aircraft
- Modern war planes
- Flight and the atom bomb
- The future of flight

Music

- Songs and music about flight

Art

- Bird flight patterns
- Airline insignia
- Aeroplane paintings
- Make and decorate a kite
- Model aircraft
- Make your own passport

English

- A day in the life of an airport
- Preparing for take-off
- Role play – airport life
- The alphabet of the air – the language of pilots in flight
- Ancient myths and legends about flight
- Flight stories
- Cayley's coachman
- 'Airspeak'
- Historical newspapers

Mathematics

- Breaking the sound barrier
- Jet speed records
- The cost of air travel

Geography

- Airport plans
- Immigration and customs controls
- Flight routes and destinations
- Bird migration journeys

BASIC CONCEPTS ▶

1 Many things are able to fly through the air: some of these are 'natural' fliers from the world of animals, birds and insects, whilst others are man-made craft, powered to fly by a variety of sources.

2 Forces are necessary to enable all aircraft to take off, land and fly through the air.

3 Flight is important to our world for a wide variety of reasons. It gives people pleasure and has many practical uses.

4 **Note**: Little is said about space flight in this topic, since this is covered in the topic on 'Space', p. 135. Activities from both topics could well be combined into a topic on space flight.

STARTING POINTS ▶

● Make a collection of photographs or other pictures of things that fly, including a wide range of species from the world of animals, birds and insects as well as machines.

● Visit an airport. Contact the airport to see whether it is possible for the children to visit. Make a preliminary reconnaissance visit yourself, of course, to collect as much information as possible about the airport, airlines, flight schedules, etc.

● Go outdoors and look up ... watch the sky ... see if you can see anything flying ... try to identify it ... ask the basic question: why doesn't it fall out of the sky?

SCIENCE/TECHNOLOGY ▶

Activity 1: Lots of things can fly ...

● 'Brainstorm' the word 'flight'–ask the children to write a list of all the things they can think of that can fly, then to share this list with the class; or go round the class and ask each child in turn to name something that can fly. This can even be done as an elimination game, with the winner being the one who can name the most flying things. The list should be long: owl, butterfly, dragonfly, bee, fly, wasp, jumbo jet, robin, bat, swallow, Concorde, helicopter, etc. This activity should lead to interesting discussion and help to clarify exactly what

we mean by flying. Do not, for example, accept an answer of 'bird', since some birds such as the penguin and the kiwi do not fly. Decide whether you will include such things as 'kite', 'hot air balloon' and 'glider', and discuss how these are different from aircraft. Make a distinction between 'natural' fliers–birds, insects, etc.– and machines that fly as a result of the application of science and technology to non-living materials.

● Make a class collection of pictures of things that fly cut from magazines. Let the children cut these out, then arrange them into sets of things from the natural

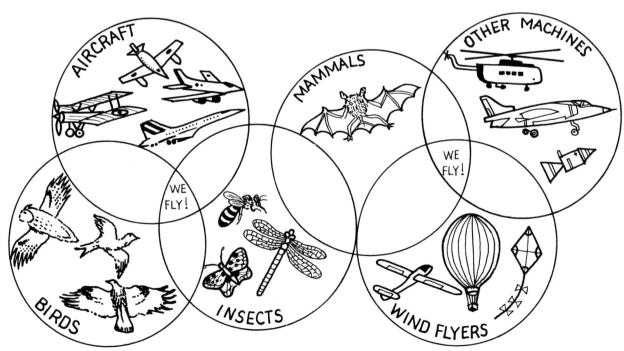

44

world and flying 'machines'. A similar activity could be undertaken by asking the children to draw flying things, then cutting out their drawings and arranging them into sets. Depending on the age of the children, the sets could be made more complex, for example, by separating 'natural' fliers into insects, birds and mammals, and other flying objects into aircraft, wind-powered flyers and other machines such as helicopters and spacecraft.

Activity 2: About aircraft

● Use **Copymaster 1** to help children learn the names of the key parts of a modern aircraft. This knowledge is required for a more in-depth understanding of how planes fly and the general operation of aircraft and airports. The Copymaster shows an aircraft and a set of jumbled names for the children to read and then fit into the appropriate label boxes. The correct answers are:

1. rudder
2. elevator
3. passenger door
4. aileron
5. engine
6. wing
7. flaps
8. main wheels
9. fuselage
10. cockpit
11. nose
12. nose wheels
13. spoilers
14. tailplane

● Extend the above activity by preparing work cards about each of these plane parts, illustrating each, and asking the children to write a sentence explaining the importance of each.

Background information
The rudder is used to make the plane turn to the left or to the right. Wing flaps open out from the wings when the plane takes off, helping it to become airborne. The elevators move up and down to help the plane climb up or dive in the air. The engine enables it to move and travel through the air. The ailerons on the back edge of the wings help the plane to fly level, and they can be tilted to make the plane turn corners. The spoilers are fixed to the top of the wing, and can be tilted up to make the wings tip forwards so that the plane goes down.

● Discuss the parts of a plane that are necessary to make it fly in different directions: the flaps, elevators, ailerons, rudder and spoilers are all moving parts of the wings and tail. The pilot uses controls on the flight deck to move these as required.
● Discuss the parts necessary to help lift the plane into the air and enable it to come down and land – the flaps, spoilers and wheels. Note, of course, the essential function of the engine, which enables the plane to move.

Activity 3: The forces of flying

● Use **Copymaster 2** to help the children learn about how planes fly. As it moves through the air, four forces keep the aircraft flying level. After further research and discussion, ask the children to write the names of these four forces in the appropriate arrow boxes on the Copymaster, colour the picture, and perhaps write an account of how planes fly, taking account also of the following activity.

Background information
The four forces are **drag, lift, thrust** and **weight**. Drag is the force of air pushing against the plane when it is flying forwards: in other words, it is the air's resistance to an aircraft moving through it. Weight is a force pulling down on the plane, balancing its lift. Thrust is the force produced by the engines that pulls the plane forwards through the air. Lift is the force produced by air rushing over the top of the wings that pushes the plane up from below. Explain to the children that air itself is an important factor in flight, linking this to the following activity. Air is moving around all the time, and it has weight. A plane stays up in the air because air is rushing past its wings.

● Provide thin strips of paper for the children to conduct an air pressure experiment. Suggest that they hold a strip close to their lips and blow over the top of it. Watch what happens – the paper will rise because there is less air on top of the paper, and so the air underneath pushes it upwards.

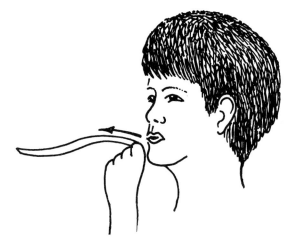

What happens when you blow air over the paper?

Explain that this is a much simplified version of what happens with aircraft wings. Wings are flat on their underside and curved on top. As an aircraft flies, air flows further and faster over the curved upper surface than over the flat under surface and so the air pressure there is less than that below the wings. (The air is more 'spread out' over the upper surface: see diagram on page 47.) Therefore the stronger air pressure below causes the plane to move up. This is how a plane takes off from the ground. Help the children to appreciate that flying an aeroplane is of course very much more complex than moving a piece of paper upwards; and that, as already discussed, a plane has to be able to turn, climb and swoop down in the sky – hence the many hinged parts to its wings and tail which the pilot is trained to operate as necessary.

Activity 4: Power for flight

● Explore the sources of power which enable machines to stay in the air. Perhaps small groups of children could investigate and produce illustrated accounts of the flight power of various crafts, which can then be assembled as part of an overall flight frieze. Some examples are shown overleaf.

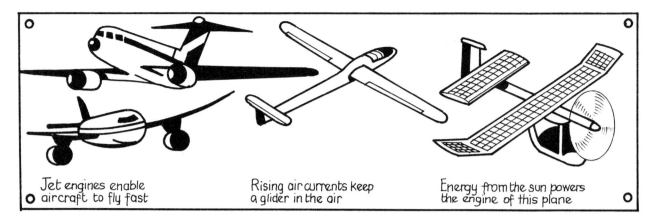

Jet engines enable aircraft to fly fast

Rising air currents keep a glider in the air

Energy from the sun powers the engine of this plane

Power for flight

- Consolidate the above activity by using **Copymaster 3** which shows a range of craft that fly and some power sources. Ask the children to colour the craft, identify and label them, then draw a line linking each to its appropriate power source.
- Older children can be helped with resources to find out more about the development and operation of aircraft engines, and perhaps assisted in drawing annotated diagrams of a modern, kerosene engine.

Background information

Modern aircraft are powered by jet engines. The earliest engines operated with pistons and ran on petrol. The engine turned a propeller which caused the plane to be pulled forwards through the air. A modern engine burns the fuel kerosene, which produces hot gases. These are thrust out of the engine's exhaust at great speed, while new air is sucked in by the engine at the front. In this way, the aeroplane is pushed forwards through the air.

- Demonstrate how expelled air has the power to move an object by using balloons. Let the children blow up a balloon, and then hold the neck so that the air is trapped inside. Let go ... and watch the balloon shoot forwards through the air, powered by the air rushing out of its neck. This is a much simplified version of jet power!

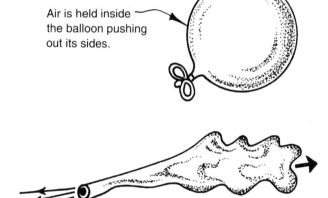

Air is held inside the balloon pushing out its sides.

Air is released, the balloon shoots forward and shrinks in size.

A simple demonstration of the principle of jet propulsion

- For younger children who are not yet able to construct their own diagrams, provide an outline cutaway drawing of a jet engine, based on the diagram below, and a series of 'glossary' work cards with related

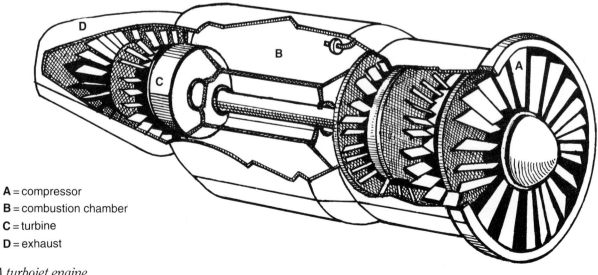

A = compressor
B = combustion chamber
C = turbine
D = exhaust

A turbojet engine

terms and explanations of them. Ask the children to label the correct parts of the engine.

Labels suitable for work cards relating to the above activity may include:

- **A Compressor:** a series of blades shaped like aerofoils (see next activity) which turn very fast and pull air into the engine. This air soon becomes heated.
- **B Combustion chamber:** fast-travelling, heated air passes into a combustion chamber where it mixes with the fuel kerosene. The mixture of air and kerosene is lit by a spark so that it explodes, producing hot gases.
- **C Turbine:** hot gases from the combustion chamber turn turbine blades round. The turbine then turns the compressor, which continues to suck new air into the engine, thus keeping the engine running.
- **D Exhaust:** hot gases are forced past the turbine and rush at an extremely fast pace out of the engine's tail-pipe. This expulsion of air is in part responsible for the loud noise which jet aircraft make as they fly.

● Introduce the word 'aerofoils', which is needed for an explanation of the concept of flight. An aerofoil is something that is shaped so as to create lift when it moves through the air; for example, the wing of an aircraft. Blades in an aircraft engine's compressor are also shaped like aerofoils. The diagram above right, which could be reproduced for or by the children, shows a sideways view of an aerofoil and the pattern of air flowing around it.

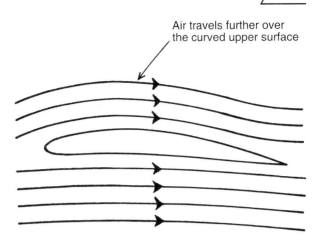

Air travels further over the curved upper surface

Air pressure is higher beneath the flat surface and therefore the aerofoil rises

An aerofoil

● Discuss why power is necessary for flight – while this may seem obvious, the children may not have thought through the idea that any object heavier than air will fall to the ground because of the force of gravity.

Activity 5: Why is flight important to us?
● Go round the class asking children to suggest reasons why flight is important and useful to us. Make a list of these reasons, and then develop this activity into a patchwork style display, made up of rectangles which illustrate and explain the reasons. Children could work in pairs to complete a box for the display.

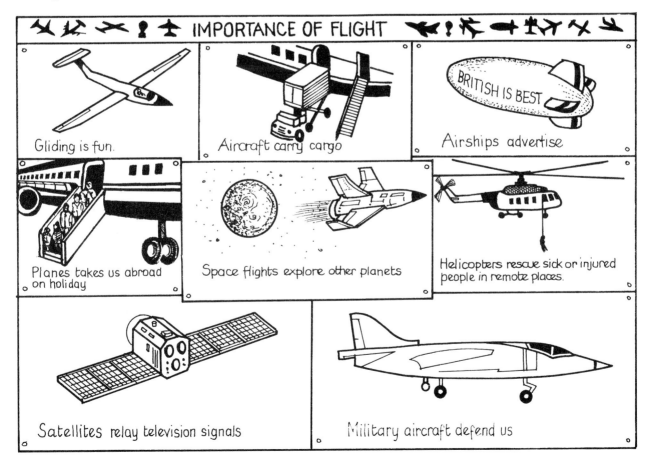

IMPORTANCE OF FLIGHT

Gliding is fun.

Aircraft carry cargo

Airships advertise

Planes takes us abroad on holiday

Space flights explore other planets

Helicopters rescue sick or injured people in remote places.

Satellites relay television signals

Military aircraft defend us

Activity 6: About helicopters

● Find out about how helicopters can use vertical take-off and landing techniques, and hover in one place in the air. Investigate some of the many useful functions that helicopters fulfil. Use **Copymaster 4** as a basis for recording knowledge about helicopters. Children can colour the top half of the Copymaster, then design an exciting lower half to complete the picture. Ask them to use their imaginations to think up a suitable scenario for what the helicopter might be doing. Some sentences could be added to explain briefly the situation chosen, though each child can write a full story elsewhere about his or her picture. More technical writing can also be undertaken to explain how helicopters take off, hover and land.

Background information

Helicopters can gain access to sites that cannot be reached in any other way, and the capacity to achieve vertical take-off, to hover and to land make them ideal for specialist uses such as sea and mountain rescue, the delivery of heavy loads to confined spaces, transportation to isolated sites such as oil rigs, security watches, crop spraying and medical missions to remote locations.

Helicopters get lift and thrust from spinning wings called rotor blades, which are driven by an engine. When the rotor blades spin round fast and are kept level, the helicopter hovers in one spot in the air. When the blades are tilted down at the front, the air is pushed back, and the machine moves forward. When the rotor blades are tilted back, air is pulled in front of the machine and it moves backward. A rotor on the tail controls movement of the helicopter to the right and left. The rotor blades are shaped like aerofoils.

The first successful helicopter was flown in Germany (1937), and in 1939 its performance was surpassed by the 'Sikorsky', an American machine designed by and named after a Russian who had emigrated to the USA in 1919.

Activity 7: 'Lighter-than-air' craft

● Make a special study of the science and technology of craft that are lighter-than-air, and are therefore capable of flying. Such craft do not have aerofoil wings, but depend on hot air or gases to lift them off the ground and into the air. This activity could lead on to a sub-topic on 'air', as the children will need to understand some physical properties of air in order to learn how lighter-than-air craft operate. A key concept is that hot air is lighter than cool air: hence, when a balloon is filled with hot air, it will rise off the ground. Find pictures of hot-air balloons and explain how they function.

Background information

Balloons were the very first form of air transport. The earliest ones were filled with hot air, while later versions used hydrogen gas, which is 14 times lighter than air. A gas burner is used to blow hot air into a hot-air balloon. The air is kept hot with a series of bursts of flame so that the balloon stays afloat. The direction of the wind decides which way the balloon will travel. When it is

time to descend, the pilot allows the air inside the balloon to cool, so that the craft gradually drops safely to the ground.

● A large collage picture of a colourful hot-air balloon will make a splendid centrepiece for a wall display on 'Flying – lighter-than-air'. Label the balloon parts, and incorporate pictures and descriptions of other craft which use lighter-than-air technology, such as airships. Mention pioneers such as Sir George Cayley, Henri Giffard, Count Zeppelin in Germany, and the R101 airship disaster in 1930.

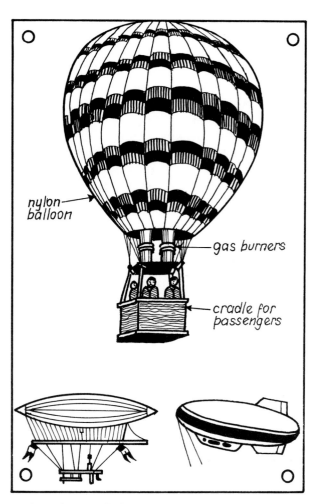

Lighter-than-air flight

Activity 8: Kites

● The power of the wind can be demonstrated by flying kites. Let the children design and construct kites in a variety of shapes, and investigate which designs are the most successful in the air. This activity obviously requires a windy day for experimentation with finished products, and if possible a good open space so that the children can fly their kites as high as possible.

Background information

The children may be interested to learn that the Chinese developed kite flying. They also invented gunpowder which was used to power 'flying rockets' which were equipped with curved knives and fired at an enemy in battle.

Activity 9: Gliders and parachutes

• Investigate other, more sophisticated craft which fly by wind power, such as gliders, hang gliders and parachutes. Again, collage pictures of these will make a colourful wall display, together with descriptions of how they function. Diagrams can be drawn to show how a glider flies, powered by rising warm air currents which spiral upwards. The skills of being a good glider pilot depend on finding these thermal currents and helping the glider to remain 'on the up' with the spiralling air.

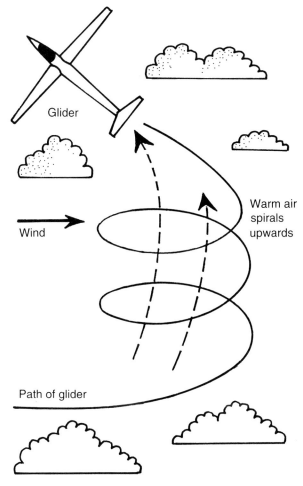

Gliders use rising thermal air currents

Activity 10: The flight of birds

• Compare 'natural flight' with that of aircraft. Discuss why humans cannot fly while birds can. Birds are able to stay up in the air because of the 'lift' generated when their aerofoil-shaped wings move forwards. As the wings move up and down, they provide 'thrust' and the bird's body is propelled through the air.

• If possible, take the children outdoors into open spaces and watch birds fly. Observe flight patterns, and note whether birds are flying in straight or curved pathways, singly or in groups. Sketch patterns observed.

Background information

Some birds, such as ducks, tend to fly in a straight line. Some, like the chaffinch, go up and down in the air; others, like the buzzard, soar in a spiralling path, resembling the pathway of a glider. Indeed, soaring birds with large wings depend on rising thermals of air to take them spiralling up into the air, in the same way that gliders do.

• Take a careful look at bird wing feathers, perhaps collected on a woodland walk, and preferably under a microscope. Make sketches of feathers, and explain their structure in diagrammatic form.

Background information

The flight feathers or remiges of a bird are those feathers in the wings that are used in flight. They consist of long, strong main feathers (primaries) and shorter, less prominent feathers (secondaries). Each feather is a light structure made of a substance called keratin. It has a central shaft or rachis, with thinner filaments called barbs. In turn, the barbs have tiny filaments called barbules. The barbules interlock, making a flat air-resistant surface as the wing pushes the air backwards but letting air through as the wing comes forward again.

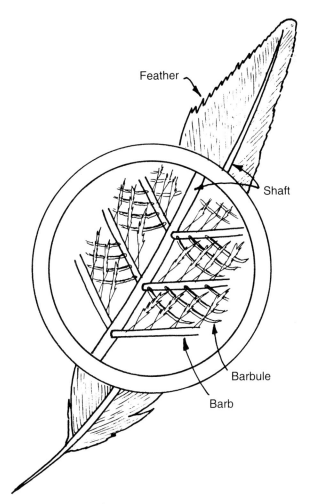

Examine a bird's feather under a microscope

• Ask the children to suggest reasons and write about why birds fly. Their various reasons could be written out and displayed with related paintings. Alternatively, prepare a series of pictures such as those suggested overleaf, and let children think of suitable captions for them.

WE FLY.......

To go to warmer places in winter

To escape enemies on the ground

To search for food on land or sea

To catch food in the air

To build nests high up in safe places

To find safe places to rest

- Talk about how birds take off and land. Take-off is achieved by rapid flapping of the wings, causing lift. To slow down when landing, a bird puts out its feet and spreads out its tail and wings.
- Make a book or display entitled 'Natural Flight', with illustrations and writing about animals, birds and insects. Specific varieties could be investigated (for example, butterflies, bats, dragonflies) and certain birds focused upon – perhaps those with particularly large or interestingly shaped wings. During this activity, bear in mind that the focus of the study is on flight, so children should pay particular attention to wing size, shape, colour and action, as well as individual flight patterns and reasons for flying in each case.

MATHEMATICS

Activity 11: Breaking the sound barrier
- Discuss what is meant by the term 'breaking the sound barrier', and research flight statistics of various aircraft that have been able to do this. This activity has a historical dimension, and could be linked to a study of the development of aircraft through the ages. Suggest that the children construct a display of their paintings of aircraft noted throughout history for their speed, and make an accompanying table of speeds.

Background information
The speed of sound (Mach 1) is 1223 km/h (760 miles per hour), at sea level. At higher altitudes, sound travels more slowly. At 11 000 m (36 000 feet) Mach 1 is 1062 km/h (660 mph). The term Mach derives from the name of the Austrian scientist (Dr Ernst Mach, 1838–1916) who first calculated sound speeds.

In the 1940s, fighting planes travelled at top speeds of around 864 km/h (525 mph). By the 1950s Britain's Canberra and V-bombers and a number of foreign planes had attained speeds of over 965 km/h (600 mph).

Supersonic (faster than sound) flight began in 1953 with the American F-100 Super Sabre and the Russian MiG-19 aircraft reaching speeds of around 1.4 Mach. The Franco-British Concorde, the world's fastest passenger airliner which began services to North America in 1976, flies at 2333 km/h (1450 mph) or 2.04 Mach – over twice the speed of sound – when cruising at high altitude. The United States Air Force jet, Lockheed SR-71, travelled at 3529.5 km/h (2193.2 mph), Mach 3.5, and the North American X-15 has achieved a flight speed of Mach 6.0.

- Help the children to research jet speed records, by providing suitable reference material from books of records, encyclopaedias and books on the history of jet aircraft.
- Investigate the cost of present-day air travel. Take selected airlines and routes, for example, a British Airways flight from London to New York; a Delta flight from London to Atlanta; an Iberia flight from London to Rio de Janeiro; and ascertain the cost of these from a travel agent. If time and the patience of the travel agents allow, seek alternative costings and consider why some flights are less expensive than others when the same (or even greater) distance is covered. This activity could also lead to finding out about the different costs of various classes of travel – economy, club class and executive class, or whatever terminology a particular airline uses. Make work cards on flight costs, asking children to calculate the cost of, for example, taking a family on a certain air route, given basic costings per person.

ART

Activity 12: Flight-pattern pictures
● Make bird flight-pattern pictures, including flight paths as observed in the field or learned from secondary resources. Include the silhouettes of the birds who created them.

Birds have different flight patterns

Activity 13: Airline insignia
● Paint pictures of the insignia of some of the world's leading airlines. These would make a colourful border for a wall display on flight or passenger travel. Travel agency brochures will be a valuable source of information for this activity.

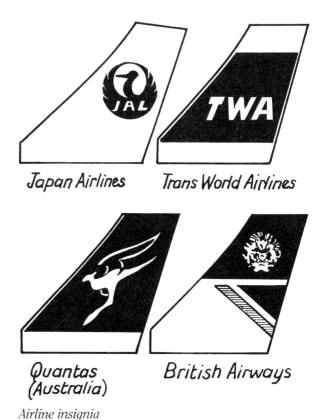

Airline insignia

HISTORY

Activity 14: The history of flight
● Make a class book entitled 'The History of Flight'. Perhaps children can be divided into small groups to research, write about and illustrate different periods and achievements. Tell the children of the early bird-men of medieval times – Oliver the Mad Monk of Malmesbury, for example, who jumped from the west tower of the Abbey in AD1000 and survived, although lame for the rest of his natural days (an ideal subject for a historical newspaper). The following background material on the earliest days of flying may be useful in providing suggestions for further research on this period.

Background information
Leonardo da Vinci (1452–1519), the great Italian inventor and artist, had drawn sketches of flying machines towards the end of the fifteenth century, including what appear to have been ideas for a helicopter and a parachute, but no prototypes were ever launched. However, the first successful flying invention was the hot-air balloon pioneered by the Montgolfier brothers in France. In summer 1783 a large balloon made of linen and paper rose to a height of 6000 feet before returning safely to earth, and on 21 November, 1783, two passengers rose to a height of 3000 feet, travelling $5\frac{1}{2}$ miles and once again landing safely. Next came the hydrogen balloon; the first flight was made from Paris in 1783 by Jaques Charles. During a famous flight by Frenchman Jean Blanchard and an American, Dr Jeffries, in 1785, the balloon began losing height: Blanchard and Jeffries had to throw out much of the contents of the passenger basket to stay in the air, including most of their clothes! Fortunately, the balloon landed safely in France.

In 1874, Felix du Temple attempted the world's first powered flight in a monoplane, but travelled only a very short distance. In 1890, Clement Ader became the first person to lift himself off the ground in a self-propelling flying machine.

On 17 December 1903, the American Wright brothers, Wilbur (1867–1912) and Orville (1871–1948), made the first true powered aeroplane flight at Kitty Hawk in North Carolina, USA. They had become interested in flying in the 1890s and at first built gliders. Their famous original flying machine – known as the Flyer – was powered by a petrol engine, mounted on the plane's lower wing, which drove two pusher propellers. The machine flew under its own power for 40 yards. A flickering old newsreel film of this original flight is still in existence, and should be shown to the children if at all possible. This is what the Wright brothers wrote about their first successful flight:

> 'This flight lasted for only twelve seconds but it was nevertheless the first in the history of the world in which a machine carrying a man had raised itself into the air in flight, had sailed forward without a reduction in speed and had finally landed at a point as high as that from which it had started.'

In actual fact, the brothers made two flights each on that special day in aviation history. The final flight lasted for 59 seconds and covered a distance of 852 feet.

The original Wright *Flyer* was soon replaced by versions 2, 3 and 4. *Flyer 3* stayed airborne for 38 minutes and covered a distance of 39 kilometres (24 miles). Several versions of the fourth *Flyer* were built, and one was even flown by Wilbur Wright in European skies.

Shortly after the Wright brothers' success, pioneering work was undertaken in Europe. Alberto Santos-Dumont became the first European to fly more than 25 m (80 feet) in 1906, and in 1908 Mr S.F. Cody made the first official flight in Britain, covering 496 yards at a height of between 50 and 60 feet.

In May 1909, Cody became the first person to fly over a mile in Britain, and in July 1909 Louis Blériot made the first cross-Channel aeroplane flight in a Type XI monoplane. The flight lasted for 37 minutes. In the same year, the Wright brothers sold the US army its first aeroplane, and the first Aviation Display took place at Rheims, in France, with 38 different aircraft taking part.

Activity 15: Famous aviators …
- Research some 'famous pioneers of flight', and link the names of aviators with the aircraft, special events in their lives and appropriate dates. Include the names of Sir George Cayley, an Englishman, and German Otto Lilienthal, who both built and flew gliders in the latter half of the nineteenth century. Others worthy of mention include de Havilland, Frenchman Henri Giffard (first successful flight in a power-driven airship at a speed of 6 mph in 1852), Alcock and Brown (first flight across the North Atlantic in June 1919, lasting 16 hours and 12 minutes), A.V. Roe, Ross Smith (flight from London to Australia in 1919), Sir Charles Cobham who flew to South Africa and back in 1925, and Charles Lindbergh, who completed the first solo crossing of the Atlantic in $33\frac{1}{2}$ hours in 1937.

Activity 16: … and a famous aviatrix or two
- Tell or research the story of Amy Johnson (1903–1941).

Background information
Until the 1920s, flying was strictly a male preserve. Gradually, however, opportunities began to arise for women to learn to fly, though there was much prejudice against such interlopers for many years. Women like Amy Johnson had to apply themselves with great dedication if they were to succeed. In fact, within two years of starting to fly, Amy was preparing for a solo flight to Australia (1930). The flight took 19 days to complete, and Amy herself undertook much of the servicing and repairing of the aircraft (a Tiger Moth called the *Jason*). Bad weather and accidents lost her the chance of setting a new record for the flight, but she received a rapturous reception on her arrival at Darwin. Afterwards, Amy Johnson even had a popular song, 'Amy, Wonderful Amy', written in her honour. If possible, play a recording of the song to the children once they have heard her story.

- Find out more about Amelia Earhart (1898–1937), another famous aviatrix, whose story ends in a mystery which has never been solved. Perhaps the children could speculate on what might have happened.

Background information
Amelia Earhart, an American social worker, gained her pilot's licence in 1923. She was the first female aviator to reach an altitude of 14 000 feet (1924), and had experimented with air-cooled engines. Together with a well known pilot named Wilbur Stultz, she set out from Newfoundland in a three-engined aircraft called *Friendship* on 17 June 1928, in another bid to cross the Atlantic. Despite air storms, ice forming on the wings and misfiring engines, the plane struggled across the ocean and finally landed in Wales. When Amelia stepped out of the aircraft, her only luggage was a logbook recording the story of the flight, a comb and a toothbrush.

Amelia's impressions of the flight swiftly became a best seller, particularly with descriptions such as 'clouds like fantastic gobs of mashed potatoes'. In the years that followed, Amelia continued her pioneering work: she tested new engines and aircraft and flew autogyros, the predecessors of the modern helicopter, when they were still in the experimental stage. In May 1932 she flew the Atlantic alone, the first woman to do so. Once again, the flight was dogged by danger (thunderstorms, a small fire in the cockpit, ice on the wings, malfunctioning instruments, a leak in the lead to the fuel gauge), and once again Amelia battled on until she landed in Ireland. The flight had taken 14 hours and 56 minutes, another flying record for the intrepid aviatrix. At this time, the American Charles Lindbergh was the most celebrated airman in the world, and Amelia's achievements soon gained her the nickname of 'Lady Lindy'.

In 1935, Amelia became the first woman to fly across the Pacific Ocean from Honolulu to California, a distance of 2500 miles. Two years later, came her greatest undertaking so far – a plan to fly around the world with an expert navigator, Fred Noonan, in a twin-engined Lockheed Electoral monoplane called the *Lady Lindy*. The flyers flew for 23 000 miles and landed for refuelling in New Guinea. The final stage of the journey was the 2500 miles between New Guinea and the tiny Howland Island in the Pacific Ocean. It was on that final stage that the *Lady Lindy* vanished without trace. Amelia Earhart and Fred Noonan were never seen again, despite a thorough search by ships of the US Navy on the orders of President Roosevelt himself. There have been a number of theories as to how two such experienced flyers were lost, including one speculation that Earhart and Noonan were spying for America against the Japanese, who were at that time thought to be preparing secret naval bases in the Pacific Islands. It was rumoured that the two flyers had been captured by the Japanese, and had died or been executed in captivity. To this day, the mystery has never been solved.

● Ask the children to think about the following quotation, taken from a well known columnist's epitaph for Amelia Earhart. Walter Lippmann wrote that:

'The world is a better place to live in because it contains human beings who will give up ease and security and stake their own lives in order to do what they themselves think worth doing. They do the useless, brave, noble, divinely foolish and the very wisest things that are done by man … And what they prove to themselves and to others is that man is no mere creature of his habits, no mere automaton in his routine, but that in the dust of which he is made there is also fire, lighted now and then by great winds from the sky.'

Activity 17: A flight timeline
● Begin an illustrated timeline of flight. This can be started early in the topic and added to as work progresses. Add dates of importance in aviation history and the development of flight techniques, illustrated with sketches of relevant people and aircraft. This timeline could be built up across the length of a classroom wall. Use **Copymaster 5** as a basis for the individual pupil's own record of key events in history. As individual research and reading progresses, each child can add to his/her own timeline before transferring the information to the large timeline wall display. The Copymaster shows a number of key dates as starting points for elaboration.
● Make a special study of military aircraft, perhaps focusing on the craft used in World Wars I and II. They include the Sopwith Camel, the Hawker Hurricane, the Supermarine Spitfire, the Gloster Meteor and the Hawker Typhoon. Famous heavy bombers of the Second World War built in Britain include the Avro Lancaster, the Handley Page Halifax, the Vickers-Armstrong Wellington and the DH Mosquito.

Background information
During World War I the concept of 'air power' was still in its infancy. Early planes of that period were not designed to carry weapons and had open cockpits. Flyers would shoot at each other with revolvers, and aircraft were used to photograph battlefields, and to drop hand grenades and explosives on enemy territory. The results were often wildly inaccurate!

The years following World War I saw the rapid development of all kinds of aircraft. Many new planes were built and put into service: some were armed with heavy machine guns, while others were specialist bombers. By the time of World War II, planes were a crucial aspect of both attack and defence. Heavily armed fighters had been developed which could carry bombs and other weapons.

The wartime years once again brought a dramatic improvement in the qualities and the capabilities of aircraft, particularly with the development of electronic systems, radar and aircraft carrier warfare. The first jet aircraft to fly (May 1941) was the Gloster-Whittle E28/39, designed by Sir Frank Whittle. The first British jet fighter was the Gloster Meteor (1944), and the first British jet-propelled bomber was the Canberra (1949). The Canberra was the first plane to fly from London to New York and back in one day. The design of aircraft changed drastically because of the very high altitudes at which these aircraft flew, and pressurised cabins had to be introduced.

Activity 18: Wartime paintings
● Let the children paint wartime paintings, of famous fighter or bomber aircraft flying over a townscape or the countryside. A painting of a Spitfire, for example, would look very effective set against a painted backcloth of patchwork fields and hedgerows, depicting the English landscape – a contrast between war and peace.

Spitfire over England!

Activity 19: Famous air battles of World War II
● Read and write about some of the famous air battles of World War II, including the Battle of Britain, the attack on Pearl Harbor by the Japanese in 1941, the German Blitz of Britain (1940) and the Battle of Midway between Japan and the USA (1942).

Activity 20: Hiroshima and Nagasaki
● Find out more about the significance of the dropping of the world's first atomic bombs on the

Japanese cities of Hiroshima and Nagasaki in 1945 by American B-29 Superfortress bombers. At the time, these atomic bombs were the most fearsome weapons ever to be unleashed in wartime: on 6 August, the bombing of Hiroshima resulted in the killing and wounding of 160 000 people in one explosion, and three days later a bomb dropped on Nagasaki had an equally devastating effect. On 14 August, the Japanese surrendered and World War II was over. Let the children research and write graphic accounts of these events and their repercussions, under the title 'War ends with airborne destruction', or perhaps in the form of a historical newspaper.
• Organise a debate or hold a discussion on the morality of dropping the first atomic bomb in 1945. Many of the victims of these first attacks were civilians, and many bore the scars of radioactivity for many years after the event. Were the Allied forces justified in their actions?

Background information
It has been argued that World War II would have continued in the Far East for some time, with a resultant increase in Allied casualties, had the bombs not been dropped, since the Japanese forces at that time were noted for their fanaticism.

A brief account of these events, together with graphic photographs and a facsimile of the *Daily Express* newspaper's front page of Tuesday, 7 August 1945, can be found in *Front Page History,* Harold Evan's selection of front page stories 1900–1984. The book was published in 1987 and reprinted in 1988 by Treasure Press, Michelin House, 81 Fulham Road, London, SW3 6RB. If available, the book will be a valuable resource for this and many other topics, reflecting as it does many highlights of the political and social history of the twentieth century.

Activity 21: Aircraft symbols
• Make a border to a wall display about wartime aircraft by painting the national symbols adopted by various nations in order to identify aircraft from a distance. These should include:

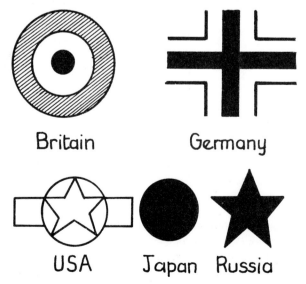

Military aircraft symbols

Activity 22: Passenger aircraft
• Detailed studies of the development of passenger aircraft could be undertaken, in particular, jet airliners, jumbos, airbuses and, of course, Concorde. Children will no doubt enjoy painting these, perhaps with cutaway sections showing the interior of the plane. The airlines themselves will be a useful source of pictures and technical information.

Background information
The first passenger air service began between London and Paris in 1925, and other services soon opened in Europe, America, Canada, Australia, the Middle East and eventually all round the world: a journey to India which would take three weeks by ship could now be completed in two days! By the end of World War II air travel had become well established: airlines and airports had sprung up in almost every country. British designers led the way in aircraft design, producing such famous aircraft as the Vickers Viscount, the Britannia, and the De Havilland Comet. In 1970, the first of Boeing's 747 jumbo jets, holding up to 550 passengers, began to compete with smaller aircraft on long-haul routes. Following this breakthrough, giant wide-bodied airbuses have been developed, including the three-jet DC10 and Lockheed Tristar, and Europe's twin-jet Airbus A300. The Airbus is noted for its ability to make very short take-offs and landings.

Activity 23: Modern-day warplanes
• Bring the historical dimension of this topic up to date by researching modern-day warplanes. Consider the great importance of flight in military defence, and the need for 'state of the art' technology. Modern, well equipped airforces are capable of carrying and delivering powerful atomic and neutron bombs; they have transport craft capable of carrying entire army divisions and weapons speedily to trouble spots or war zones, and research and reconnaissance planes equipped with sophisticated computers and related microtechnology. Military aircraft today can identify enemy targets efficiently, and kill or destroy whatever they choose with great accuracy. Organise a class debate on this situation, asking the children to express their opinions on whether flight should be used for the purposes of defence and warfare.

Activity 24: The future of flight
• Whilst this may be labelled a history section, it seems appropriate to suggest here that children should consider their ideas on the *future* of flight. This section has demonstrated the tremendous advances that have been made in aircraft design since the days of the Wright brothers, at the turn of the century. During the short wartime periods in particular, tremendous advances were made in flight technology, and modern technology continues to assist the development of ever more efficient and sophisticated craft. Ask the children to use their imaginations to design and describe aircraft of the 21st century, then to share their creations in written and illustrative forms with the rest of the class.

ENGLISH

Activity 25: A modern airport

● Write accounts of 'A Day In The Life Of A Busy Airport'. Secondary resource material will be needed to provide background information for this activity. It would be a great bonus if a visitor from your nearest airport (if one is relatively accessible) could come and talk to the children about how the place is organised, and describe all the many facets of its day-to-day operations. One way of approaching this would be to consider the groups of people who work in association with a busy airport – including aircraft crew, traffic controllers, customs officers, baggage handlers, passport officers, security staff, plane fuel carriers, mechanics, shop assistants, caterers, cleaners, bank clerks, emergency service operators and, of course, airport management staff.

A related activity drawing attention to the role and function of some of these groups of workers can be conducted in association with **Copymaster 6**. The Copymaster shows an aircraft on the ground between flights, being prepared to receive its next load of passengers. Suggest that the children colour the picture, and write accounts describing the scene and the number of essential operations that are necessary before the plane is ready for take-off. It will, of course, be helpful to talk through these operations, and anyone with extensive experience of air travel could very usefully talk to the class about pre-flight preparations. Better still, try and arrange a class visit to an airport. If this is carefully planned beforehand, then it is possible that a member of the airport staff could be available to talk to the children about airport functions. (Link with geography activities on features of an airport.)

● Role play airport life – the children could be passengers, security officials asking questions about baggage and checking hand-carried items, immigration officers, customs officials, airline representatives checking tickets and issuing boarding cards, and flight attendants seeing people safely onto the aircraft.

Done at its best, this is a complex activity: the children will need to think through the whole sequence of passing through an airport (on the way out of a country and on the way in) and act it out in the correct order. This activity links with geography – and more detailed attention to passports and customer control. You could convert the corners of your classroom into an 'airport', with security control, customs control, airline desks and a boarding area set up for role play activities. An aircraft simulation space could be established against a wall, preferably one with a long window: cover the window with black paper, and cut holes for the windows of the plane. Arrange chairs in rows adjacent to the window.

Activity 26: 'A day in the life ...'

● Ask the children to write imaginative stories about 'A Day In My Life', telling of the activities of a customs officer and/or an immigration official. These stories could be extremely humorous, telling of amusing objects found in luggage, or of 'strange' people and their attempts to smuggle themselves or other articles into the country.

Activity 27: The alphabet of the air

● Using **Copymaster 7** teach the class about the International Civil Aviation Organisation's phonetic alphabet which is used by pilots all over the world. The accepted international language of the airways is English. Discuss why such a code is needed: it is crucial that all messages between pilots and air controllers are clearly understood, and an agreed phonic alphabet is less likely to be distorted over the radio.

Provide the following words, perhaps in jumbled form, and ask the children to slot them into the correct letter space on the Copymaster:

Alpha	Juliet	Sierra
Bravo	Kilo	Tango
Charlie	Lima	Uniform
Delta	Mike	Victor
Echo	November	Whisky
Foxtrot	Oscar	X-ray
Golf	Papa	Yankee
Hotel	Quebec	Zulu
India	Romeo	

Let the children communicate with each other in 'airspeak', especially if you have a plane or airport simulation area in your classroom.

Activity 28: Flight simulation

● Schools with access to computers might be able to run a flight simulator program which enables the children to attempt to fly an aircraft. What seems at first sight to be merely a computer game could be extremely useful if used as the catalyst for accurate report writing and some understanding of the calculations and processes involved in flying.

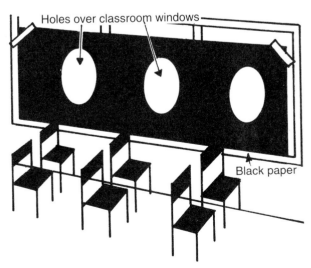

Turn the classroom into an aeroplane

Activity 29: Stories about flight

- Begin by reading or telling the children some of the myths and legends involving flight – the legends of Daedalus and Icarus, Bellerophon and Pegasus the flying horse, and Phaeton and the Horses of the Sun.
- Write stories about flying. These could be relatively factual, involving accounts of what happens on board a plane – the safety precautions, serving of food and drinks, showing of films, etc. – or they could be imaginary, telling about an exciting journey, what is seen through a plane window, new friends met on board, etc. Encourage children who have had experience of flying to describe the experience to those who have not.

There is much scope for creative writing from a historical viewpoint. For example, it is said that Sir George Cayley designed a glider in the early 1850s and compelled his somewhat reluctant coachman to act as its first pilot. The glider travelled for about a hundred yards before landing safely: the wretched coachman is said to have handed in his resignation immediately afterwards! It might be an interesting exercise for the children to relate the account of this adventure from the viewpoints of both the principal characters.

GEOGRAPHY

Activity 30: A plan of an airport

- Construct a large plan of an airport on the classroom wall, or perhaps make a model, if storage space allows. Ideally, this should be based on a genuine airport plan, perhaps obtained as the result of a visit. Alternatively, children could design their hypothetical new airport, taking account of all the necessary features, including terminal buildings (perhaps several, to cater for domestic and international flights), control tower, runways, taxiways, apron, piers, stores and aircraft hangars.

Background information

Airport runways are usually constructed so that they are parallel and in line with the prevailing winds, so that planes take off and land with the wind's assistance and are thus able to achieve greater lift. Taxiways link the main runways with the 'apron' or parking space where between-flight servicing and checking takes place. Piers link the apron and each plane's 'gate' to the terminal building. The control tower is usually in a central position, and is a hive of activity controlling all flights coming into and leaving the airport. Aircraft hangars provide shelter for parking and servicing planes, and stores and other buildings contain fuel, cargo and emergency equipment.

- Find out more about passport/immigration controls and customs operations. Show the children your own passport, and let them make one of their own, of authentic design and complete with photograph. This will be an essential piece of equipment for role playing of airport scenes (see English activities). Find out about duty free allowances relating to travel to and from Britain and other countries in the world, both inside and outside the European Community. Discuss why international travellers are bound by law to adhere to customs regulations. Investigate the penalties of failure to do so.

Activity 31: Flights from the airport

- As a result of an airport visit by the class, or by the teacher if a full outing is not possible, find out the destinations of 'flights from the airport'. Plot these on world map/s. In the case of London airports, this would of course be an exceedingly complex exercise; however, it could be narrowed down in scope by naming the various airlines operating from that airport and plotting two or three key destinations for each airline. This activity has tremendous scope for elaboration – for example, a great deal of mathematical work could be done on flight times, the lengths of routes to various parts of the world, and the costs of these flights.

Activity 32: Migration maps

- Draw maps – or plot pathways on printed maps – of the migration pathways of various birds. Discuss why birds migrate, and the fact that migration of certain species is a key reason for flying. Indeed, long flights to warmer lands save the lives of some birds who could not tolerate a cold winter. Using specialist books on the subject, try to find out how long it takes for birds to fly a certain migration route. Compare this with the time it would take an airliner to get there. As an example of an incredibly long flight, the Arctic tern flies from the Arctic all the way to South Africa or South America.

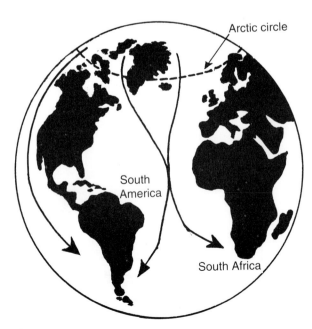

The migration route of the Arctic tern

56

MUSIC

Activity 33: 'Flying' music

• Let the children hear songs and pieces of music with aviation connections, for example:

- Vaughan Williams' 'Prelude and Spitfire Fugue', from the soundtrack music to the film *The Battle of Britain.*
- Ron Goodwin's '633 Squadron', and his soundtrack music from the film *Those Magnificent Men In Their Flying Machines,* especially the title song which makes an ideal heading for a wall display of work on those intrepid air pioneers. Indeed, the opening sequence of the film shows an amusing succession of failed attempts to fly, which might intrigue the children. Obtain a copy of the sheet music, and teach the song to the class.
- Play the Johnny Mann Singers' record of 'Up, Up And Away', the Pasadena Roof Orchestra's pastiche version of 'Me And Jane In A Plane', and if possible any version of 'Amy, Beautiful Amy'.

Parts of an aeroplane

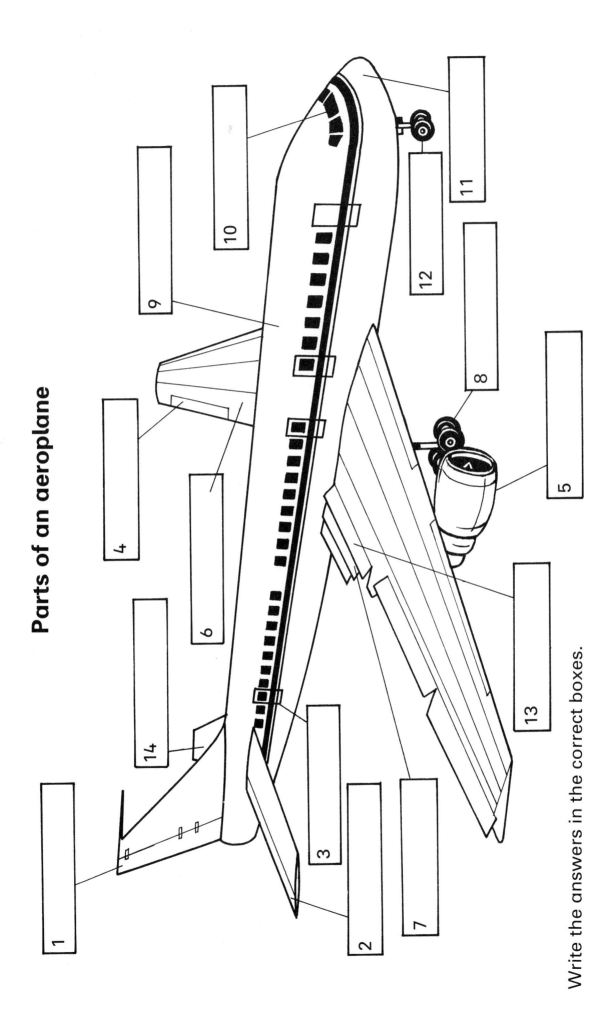

Write the answers in the correct boxes.

wing flaps, engine, rudder, cockpit, nose wheels, aileron, passenger door, spoilers, nose, elevator, wing, main wheels, fuselage, tailplane

Forces of flying

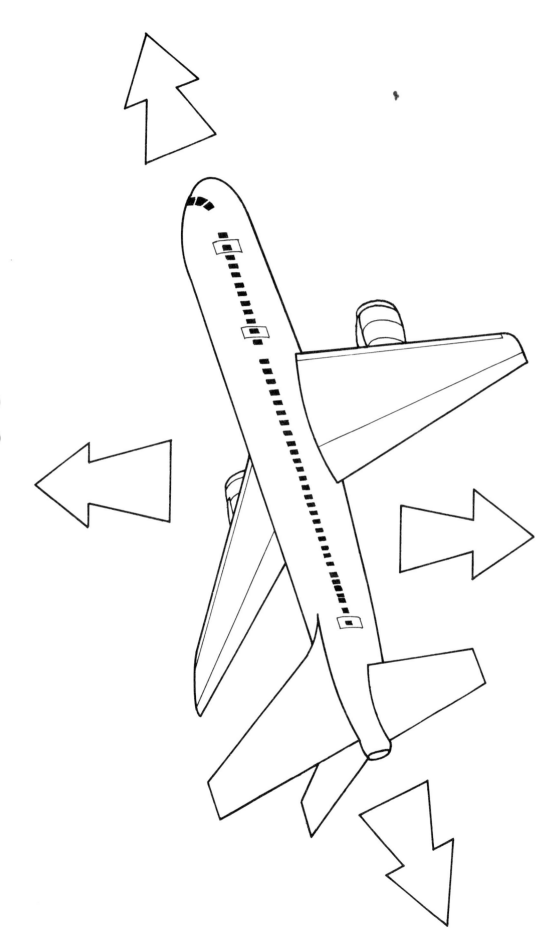

Power to fly

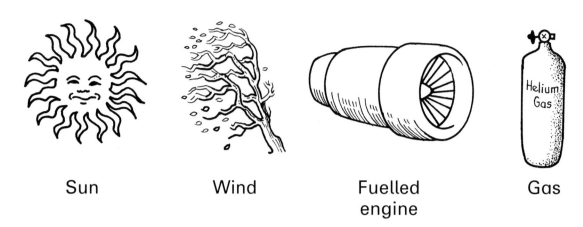

Sun   Wind   Fuelled engine   Gas

Helicopter to the rescue

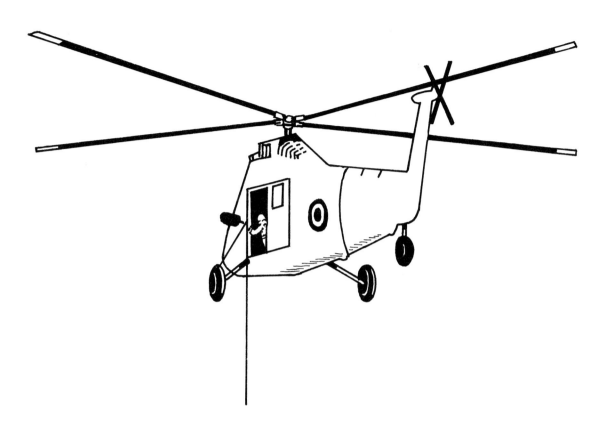

Flying through the years

1903 Wright brothers' first powered flight, Kitty Hawk, USA

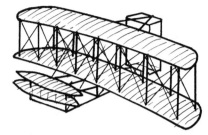

1909 Bleriot flies across the English Channel

1914 World's first passenger airline service opens, USA

1919 Alcock and Brown make first non-stop flight across Atlantic

1924 US aircraft makes first flight around the world, which took six months

1952 De Havilland Comet airlines fly first jet passenger services

1958 Boeing 707 airline comes into service

1970 Boeing 747 jumbo jet enters service with Pan American

1976 Concorde (Anglo-French) begins service to N. America

1981 First flights of new Airbus A310, Boeing 757 and 767

Ready for the flight

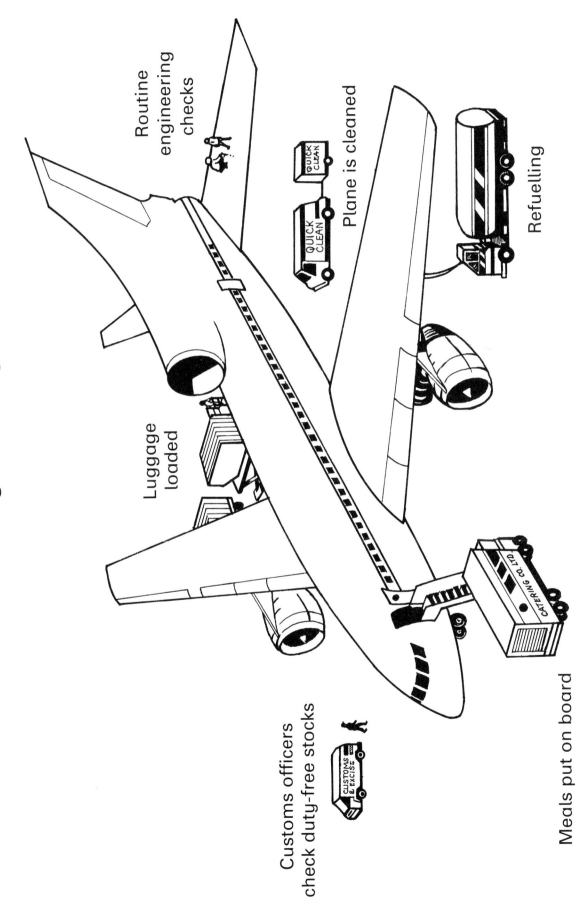

Routine engineering checks

Plane is cleaned

Refuelling

Luggage loaded

Customs officers check duty-free stocks

Meals put on board

Flight 6

Alphabet of the air

A _____   N _____

B _____   O _____

C _____   P _____

D _____   Q _____

E _____   R _____

F _____   S _____

G _____   T _____

H _____   U _____

I _____   V _____

J _____   W _____

K _____   X _____

L _____   Y _____

M _____   Z _____

Flight 7

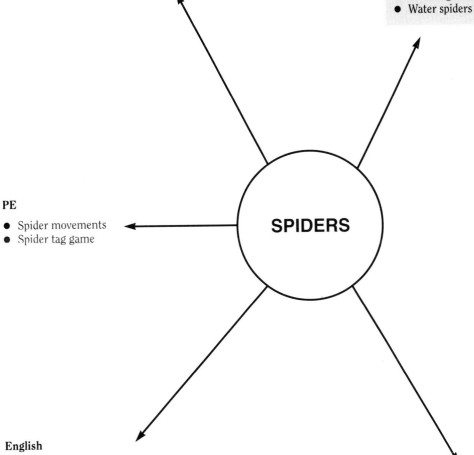

SPIDERS

Science
- Collect and observe spiders
- Study body parts
- Constructing a web
- Different kinds of web
- Alternative ways of catching prey
- Spider hunt: common native spiders
- The feeding process
- Spiders in classroom captivity
- Observe web spinning and feeding
- Preference for light and dark?
- Breeding and hatching young
- Moulting
- Water spiders

Geography
- Spiders of distant lands
- Poisonous spiders
- Keep a tarantula

PE
- Spider movements
- Spider tag game

English
- Shedding skin stories
- Spider crossword
- Spider maze puzzle
- The story of Arachne
- Other spider stories
- Superstitions
- Friendly bathroom spider

Art
- Preserve a web
- Spiders' web pictures
- Weave a web
- Make a spider board

BASIC CONCEPTS

1 Spiders belong to the group of invertebrate animals known as arachnids.

2 Usually they have simple eyes and four pairs of legs.

3 Some spiders, but not all, spin webs. Some spiders, but not all, are dangerous.

4 Spiders exist in a wide range of habitats, in the UK and around the world.

5 Many legends and stories about spiders exist around the world. Greek mythology gave the name to the spider's biological classification.

STARTING POINTS

• Find some spiders! Go out into the school grounds or nearby open space or woodland and seek some spiders to study, before returning them to their natural habitat.

• Observe spiders' webs – perhaps on a corner of a building or in the school garden. This can be done at any time of year, but is especially effective on a frosty or dewy morning, when the threads of the webs are shown up against their backgrounds.

• Make a collection of stories and poems about spiders to share with the class.

SCIENCE

C1–4

Activity 1: Take some spiders . . .

• Collect some spiders and place them in suitable containers for close observation. Clear plastic specimen pots with magnifying lids are ideal; otherwise use hand lenses. This activity could be part of a general minibeast hunt, where the children observe a variety of invertebrate creatures. Encourage them to separate out spiders from others. Many people believe that spiders are insects, which they are not; a general sorting of minibeasts will help to clarify this fact. Over a period of time, and perhaps several collections of specimens, encourage the children to identify features which are common to all spiders observed.

Use **Copymaster 1** as a recording sheet for physical features of a spider. Children can colour the drawing on this sheet in authentic colours of one of the spiders they have collected, and label the parts of the spider shown. Provide other resource material to help the children find out about the structure of a spider's body, and discuss the various body parts before they are labelled. Talk also about the title of this Copymaster, helping children to appreciate the 'family' name of spiders.

Background information
Spiders are not insects. They belong to another class of invertebrate animals known as arachnids. Other animals in this group include mites, ticks, scorpions and harvestmen.

Spiders have two main body parts: the cephalothorax (head and chest) and the abdomen. They have no wings and no antennae but have a pair of tough fangs, used to poison an enemy or to pierce food morsels. Usually spiders have eight 'simple' eyes and four pairs of legs.

The eight legs are jointed. Spiders are able to make thread, as they have silk glands which open through little holes in the body. These are called spinnerets. The silk used to make webs is sticky, so that insects become trapped in it.

• Ask the children to suggest why spiders make webs; this is of course to catch food. Discuss the 'trapping process' of the garden spider and prepare written descriptions of this to accompany web pictures in a classroom wall display.

Background information
When a web is spun by a garden spider, a line of silk is run from the web to the spider's hiding place nearby. Because a spider's eyesight is poor, it does not rely on this sense to catch insects but uses the sense of touch instead. When an insect becomes caught in the web, vibrations can be felt, and the silky thread running to the spider vibrates also. At this signal, the spider emerges to pounce on the insect trapped by the sticky web and kills it for food.

Activity 2: How does a spider spin its web?

• Investigate the technicalities of how a garden spider spins its web, and use **Copymaster 2** for the children to record the details of this process. If possible, observe a real spider in the act of performing this task; otherwise, provide a series of drawings to explain the procedure. Ask the children to complete the web drawing on the Copymaster, and to write accounts of the spinning process.

66

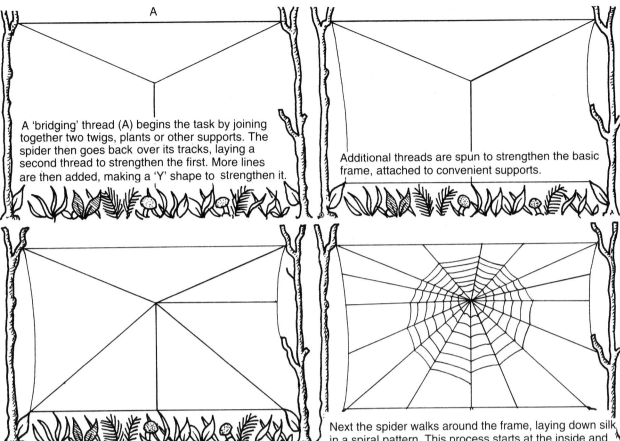

A 'bridging' thread (A) begins the task by joining together two twigs, plants or other supports. The spider then goes back over its tracks, laying a second thread to strengthen the first. More lines are then added, making a 'Y' shape to strengthen it.

Additional threads are spun to strengthen the basic frame, attached to convenient supports.

Numerous 'radii' are added to the structure, rather like spokes of a bicycle wheel. The spider is dropping and climbing all the time to achieve this.

Next the spider walks around the frame, laying down silk in a spiral pattern. This process starts at the inside and gradually works to the outside. This is the first stage of the final web. Lastly, the spider walks around the spiral again, replacing the original silk with silk-covered sticky fluid.

As the children complete the drawing on the Copymaster, remind them to include the spider …and perhaps an insect trapped in the finished web. The web which has been described and illustrated here is the 'orb' web, the web of the garden spider.

Activity 3: Different spider, different web
● Investigate the fact that different types of spiders spin different kinds of webs. Some spin webs that they sit in, others make a web attached to a hiding place by a single thread, as described above. Most spiders spin a new web every day, as the weather soon destroys a web's delicate structure. Help the children to appreciate differing shapes and structures of webs with the assistance of **Copymaster 3**, which shows four different kinds of webs. Hunt for these in appropriate places and consult further reference material about them. Ask the children to colour the webs on the Copymaster, and add an appropriate spider to each with a label to identify it. On an accompanying sheet of paper, they can write some sentences describing each of the four webs.

Background information
The orb web has already been described, and is the variety spun by a garden spider in order to catch insects.

The delicate hammock web is made by tiny black money spiders, often on lawns. Jumping and crawling insects are trapped by the web.

The tube web is spun by a wall spider, in cracks on walls. The web is shaped like a tube, and the spider hides

inside. When an insect vibrates one of the web's radial threads, the spider emerges and catches its prey, carrying it into the tube to kill and eat.

The sheet web, otherwise known as a cob web, is spun by a house spider in dark corners inside buildings such a sheds, barns and houses. The dense network of threads successfully catches insects, even though the threads are not sticky.

Activity 4: Spiders without webs?
● Find out about spiders which catch their prey without webs. Again, go out and hunt for these, and if possible sketch live specimens. The following background information provides clues about where to hunt.

Background information
Crab spiders are so called because they walk sideways like a crab. They hide in leaves or flowers, wait for an insect to come along, then pounce on it and trap it in their front legs.

The zebra spider is so called because it is black and white, like the animal. It likes to live on sunny walls, and jumps up to catch its prey. The zebra spider attaches itself to the wall with a spun thread, so that as it jumps it is prevented from falling to the ground.

Hunting spiders come out at night to search for insects. They are brown in colour, rather larger than many other spiders, and are rather fierce looking. During daylight hours, these hunting spiders shelter beneath logs or stones.

Activity 5: A spider hunt

• **Copymaster 4** provides a recording sheet for a spider hunt, showing some of the varieties of spider that may be found (not drawn to scale; some, such as the money spider, are in reality quite tiny). To complete the sheet, pupils will need to search in buildings, outdoors and in water, helping them to appreciate that spiders live in a wide range of habitats. The spiders have been labelled to help identification, but reference books will be helpful to show accurate colours and sizes. Suggest that the children colour in each spider when they have seen it, and write about where and when it was located, and what it was doing at the time (i.e. resting, walking, spinning, feeding, etc.). Any other varieties spotted can, of course, be drawn in spaces on the Copymaster or on a separate sheet of paper.

• Watch a spider feed. This may be done in a natural habitat if you have time and patience for sustained observation, or you could keep spiders for a short time in captivity (see following activity). Ask the children to write accounts of the feeding process.

Background information
Spiders catch live food to eat, and usually their prey consists of insects which are trapped in a sticky web, though some spiders pounce or jump on an unsuspecting victim. The food is first killed, by biting it repeatedly with poisonous fangs. Feeding is accomplished by sucking juices out of the insect's body. Only the empty skin or shell of the insect will remain. Often, spiders take their prey back to the web to eat, if they are not already there. A fly may be bound up in thread before it is consumed.

Activity 6: Keeping spiders in the classroom

• Collect and keep native spiders for a short time in the classroom. They should always be released after a day or two, and children should be taught why this is the case: spiders may not appear to be very attractive,

but they are living animals who should therefore always be handled with care, never tormented or hurt in any way. They should always be returned to their homes where they have the necessary food, shelter and temperature to live in a natural way. Ask the children to suggest good places to go and look for spiders – near a web is a sensible suggestion, as are in grass, flowers, leaves, under logs and stones, and in corners of dark outbuildings. Children in a school with a garden shed or bicycle shed will almost certainly not have to go far to look! Put each captured spider in a carefully prepared separate shoe box, so that it can be observed for a day or two. Provide cotton wool soaked in water with sugar for sustenance.

• Alternatively, you could construct a set of containers using cardboard lids and sheets of acetate.

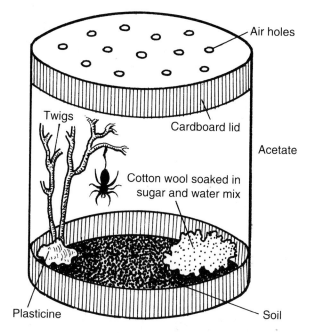

... or two cardboard lids and some acetate

• Encourage your spider to spin a web by placing a small plant or a few twigs in the container. This is best achieved in the upright-style container by 'planting' twigs in a ball of Plasticine. Twigs or even a metal coathanger could be propped up in a shoe box. Set aside time for children to gain the maximum advantage from watching the spider spin its web. They can time this process, and make detailed sketches of how it is achieved.

• Organise an experiment to see if spiders prefer light or dark resting places. Use the box-style container and cover half of the lid with black paper. Observe the box over an extended period of time to see which half the spider inhabits for various activities.

• Research the fascinating topic of how spiders breed and hatch their young. Look for cocoons and young spiders of the garden spider variety in the springtime. Search also for the rarer wolf spider, with its interesting egg sac. Suggest that the children sketch their finds, then write accounts of what they have seen, incorporating knowledge gleaned from specialist reference sources.

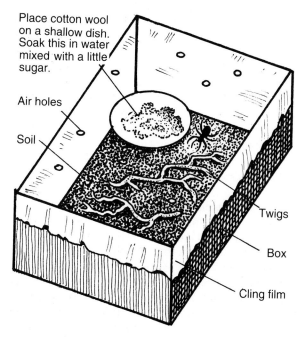

Keeping a spider in a classroom: use a box ...

Background information
Eggs of the garden spider are laid in the autumn. A cocoon of yellow thread is spun around the eggs to protect them, and the cocoon is then further protected with small pieces of twig and dead leaves. After achieving this, the female dies. The young spiders (baby spiders are called spiderlings) hatch the following spring.

Wolf spiders are not as common as house and garden spiders, but are fascinating creatures to observe if at all possible. They are brown, large in size (up to 25 mm long), have long fangs, and are fast runners. The female spins threads of silk around her eggs, and carries them around in this egg sac attached to her body. When the small spiders hatch, they are carried around on the mother's back until they can take care of themselves.

• If you are fortunate enough to find a wolf spider with an egg sac, transfer her carefully into a shoebox home and take care of her until the young hatch. Observe the spiderlings with a magnifying lens, then carefully place them outdoors in long grass with their mother.
• If possible, observe and write about the moulting process (relate to geography activities).

Background information
Newly hatched spiders are very tiny. As they grow, they shed their skin several times until they reach the size of a fully grown adult. Search for shed skins on or near spiders' webs.

• Find out more about water spiders, preferably as a result of first hand observation in ponds. Make sketches of spiders on the surface of a pond, breathing in air.

Background information
A water spider makes a web of silk attached to water plants in the pond. It breathes air, and carries bubbles of air down beneath the surface to the web. When the web is filled with air bubbles, the spider can then breathe under water. When all this air has been used up, it returns to the surface for new bubbles.

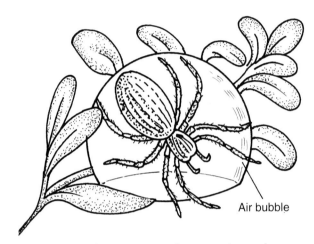

Air bubble

A water spider has its own underwater air supply

GEOGRAPHY

C5

Activity 7: Spiders from distant lands
• Investigate, using reference books, the names and habits of well known spiders from distant lands. This activity could well lead to a more general study of a foreign land, i.e. the spider in question could become a starting point for investigation of such things as climate, natural habitats and wildlife of its native country. Three obvious possible spidery starting points that will no doubt fascinate the children are the black widow spider of America, the dangerous red-back spider of Australia and the red-kneed tarantula of Mexico.

Background information
The black widow spider is one of the most dangerous spiders in the world. It is small (around 12 mm long) and bites, sometimes causing death. The red-black spider of Australia is also very dangerous. The Mexican red-kneed tarantula is deceptive, since it looks ferocious and yet is harmless. This is a large brown/black spider, some 40 mm long, with 'hairy' legs and red patches at their joints that give rise to its name.

• Use this aspect of the topic to help the children appreciate that we cannot tell whether a spider (or indeed any other animal) is dangerous merely by looking at it. Accurate identification and knowledge is necessary before we are assured that something is harmless. Explain to children that they should never handle anything alive unless they are absolutely sure that it is safe to do so. It should of course be pointed out that scientists have shown that spiders native to our own country are not dangerous to human beings, and so all of the activities suggested under the heading of 'science' are quite safe. Foreign spiders should never be acquired unless safety is assured.

Activity 8: Keeping a Mexican tarantula
• Keep a Mexican tarantula in your classroom, pointing out that it is quite harmless. Having said that, a golden rule should be that the spider is to be observed and not handled. You will need a fairly large container: a glass tank is ideal, with a bed of soil, some twigs and leaves, and a suitable hiding place for the spider – a cracked flower pot turned on its side with some dead leaves inside will be ideal. Obtain the spider from a reputable pet shop or schools' biological supplier.

Maintain humidity in the container with a mist spray filled with warm water (spray once daily) and keep the spider in a warm place (70 °F, 21 °C is ideal). Keep a dish of cotton wool soaked in sugar and water or honey and water in the container, and feed the spider with insects daily. This is, of course, a long-term project, since the specimen cannot be turned out into the wild, so before embarking upon it, check that appropriate care arrangements for the school holiday period have been made.

One of the great advantages of keeping a large spider on a long-term basis is that the children will be able to appreciate the moulting process. As the tarantula grows, it will shed its skin from time to time. This usually happens during the hours of darkness, but imagine the excitement of children coming into the classroom in the morning and seeing what appear to be two spiders side by side: the real one and its skin! Remove the skin and observe it under a microscope. Take care not to break it, as it is, of course, very delicate.

Copymaster 5 shows a large drawing of this particular variety of spider. Ask the children to colour it carefully to resemble the real thing, then write a story about a tarantula – perhaps the adventures of a tarantula in the wild in its native land; or the feelings of a victim of the tarantula as the spider approaches . . .

Find out more about tarantula spiders in their natural habitats.

Background information
The many species of tarantula found in South America and south-west USA are very large furry spiders. Many of them live in burrows. They catch insects for food. One of the biggest is the South American bird-eating spider.

ENGLISH

 C6–7

Activity 9: Shedding your skin
- Ask the children to imagine that they are a spider shedding its skin – write an imaginative poem or story about this wriggling, writhing, delicate experience.
- Use **Copymaster 6** to help teach words about spiders and their habits. Ask children to complete the crossword puzzle, then check answers and colour the background.

Background information
The solution to the crossword is:
Down: 1 zebra, 3 house spider, 4 wolf, 5 black widow.
Across: 2 sheetweb, 6 crab, 7 insects, 8 wall, 9 eyes.

- **Copymaster 7** is essentially a puzzle for enjoyment, perhaps to fill in spare minutes when other topic activities have been completed. Let pupils find the path of the spider to the fly and colour the picture.

Activity 10: Spiders in poem, song and story
- Tell the story of Arachne, a young Greek girl who gave her name to the biological class Arachnida, to which spiders belong.

Background information
According to Greek mythology, the young girl Arachne is said to have been so proud of her talent in weaving beautiful garments and tapestries that she challenged the goddess Athene, who first taught mankind how to spin and weave, to a contest of skill. One version of the tale tells that Arachne won the contest, much to the annoyance of Athene who took her revenge by turning Arachne into a spider. Another version tells that Arachne hanged herself when Athene won the contest, but the goddess brought the girl's suspended corpse to life again in the form of a spider, so that Arachne could spin unchallenged until the end of time.

- Find and read other stories about spiders – the story of Robert the Bruce, and that of *Charlotte's Web* by E.B. White (Hamish Hamilton, 1952) are two that immediately spring to mind, and the Caribbean culture contains many stories about Anansi, the Spider Man. Similar stories can also be found in the cultural traditions of West Africa.
- Find other poems and songs about spiders for the children to hear. They will probably have sung the nursery rhyme 'Incey Wincey Spider', but I doubt whether many will have heard the song of 'The Spider' included by Michael Flanders and Donald Swann on the LP *The Bestiary of Flanders and Swann* (first issued by Parlophone on PCS 3026 in 1961). If a recording is not available, it may be possible to obtain a copy of the book *The Songs of Michael Flanders and Donald Swann*, which contains the lyrics of this and many other songs. The book was compiled by Claudia Flanders, widow of Michael, and first published in 1977 by Elm Tree Books and St. George's Press.
- Consider the image of the spider, as portrayed in literature. Are they generally regarded as harmful and evil, or as helpful to human beings? Why?
- Make a list of suitable words to describe a spider, its appearance, ways of moving and so on – words such as 'scuttling', 'lurking', 'pounce', and so on. How many of these words would be complimentary?
- Let the children compose their own spider poems and imaginative stories, perhaps some in which the spider is 'friend' and others where he or she is 'foe'.
- Trace, if possible, any superstitions associated with spiders. Some people, for example, regard them as symbols of good luck with the power to cure disease, and will not remove a spider from their house if one is found there.
- A common place to find a spider in the house is in the bath tub. Discuss why this is so. Ask the children to imagine that they make friends with a spider in their bath . . . and to write about conversations held between themselves and the spider.

ART

Activity 11: Catch a spider's web
● Catch a spider's web and keep it in the classroom.

You will need:
dye (food colouring and water)
mist sprayer
a rectangle of card large enough to cover a web
glue
varnish

What to do:
Find your spider's web, and lightly spray it with dye so that it will be seen when collected and mounted. Spread glue lightly all over the card, then carefully place the card against the web. The web should affix itself to the card and come away from its twigs or other natural supports. Try and place the web centrally on the card. When the glue is dry, spray the mounted web lightly with varnish or some other fixative to strengthen it.

Note: Do not use webs that have spiders in them.

Push the card onto the web outdoors

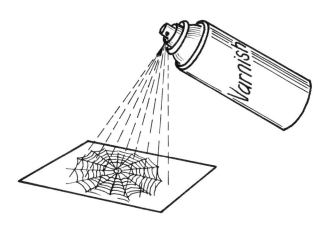

Spray the finished web with varnish to strengthen it

'Capturing' a web

Activity 12: Spider's web pictures
● Make spider's web pictures. Let each child make his/her own picture, then assemble them into a wall 'web montage'. Make a background of printed or collage leaves. Use strands of white wool to form a web shape. Glue the wool carefully onto the leaf background. Add a black felt spider and perhaps an insect to the web.

A collage spider's web makes an eye-catching display in the classroom

Activity 13: Weave a web
● Encourage the children to try and weave a web. Perhaps they could undertake this activity in pairs or

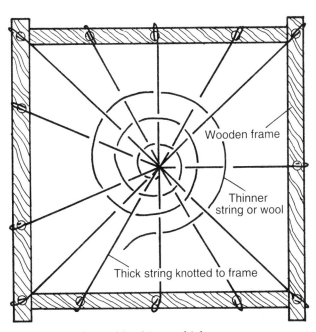

Improvise a frame like this on which to weave your own spider's web

71

groups. They will need to make a frame from thin lengths of wood, then tie thick wool or string across the frame to make the radial 'spokes'. Complete the web by weaving thinner wool or string between the spokes.

Tie a woollen 'pompom' or 3-D collage spider to the finished craftwork.

Activity 14: A spider board game
● Using the shape of a spider's web as a grid, can the children create their own simple board game? What will be the aim of such a game? Will it be an educational or a leisure game? What are the rules? If the school has access to desktop publishing facilities, it might be possible to produce polished versions of some of these games for others to play.

Background information
One such board game, 'Spider', was published in John Astrop's *Ghastly Games* (Patrick Hardy Books, an imprint of Radford Hardy Limited, 1983). If a copy can be obtained, the children could not only play this game but might be stimulated to devise one of their own.

PE ▶

Activity 14: Move like a spider
● Organise a lesson in which children imitate spiders' movements in all their forms. On all fours, let the children walk, run, 'pounce' and jump. Perhaps a web could be chalked out on the playground. Let the 'spiders' move gracefully around the threads of the web before 'pouncing' on an imaginary fly.
● Play a 'spider tag' game, where the children are spiders who chase the person 'on' (the fly) on all fours.

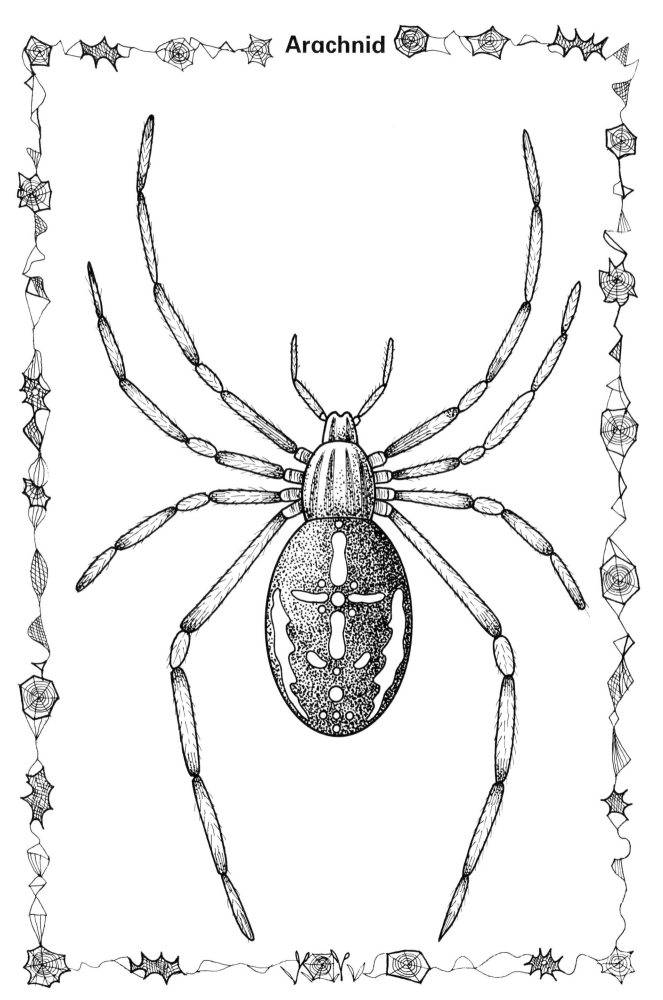

Spin a web

Webs

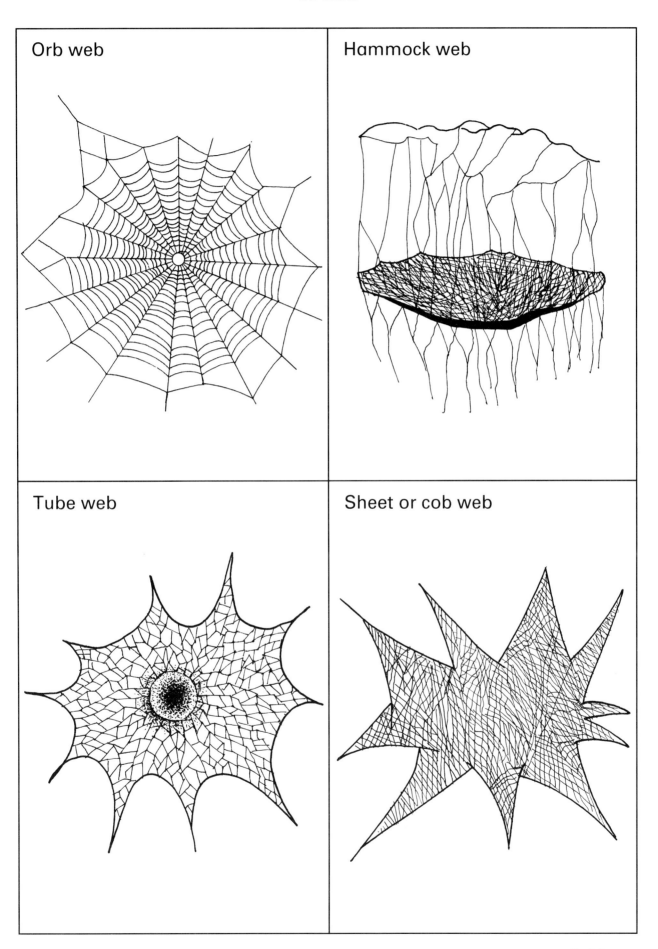

Orb web

Hammock web

Tube web

Sheet or cob web

Spider hunt

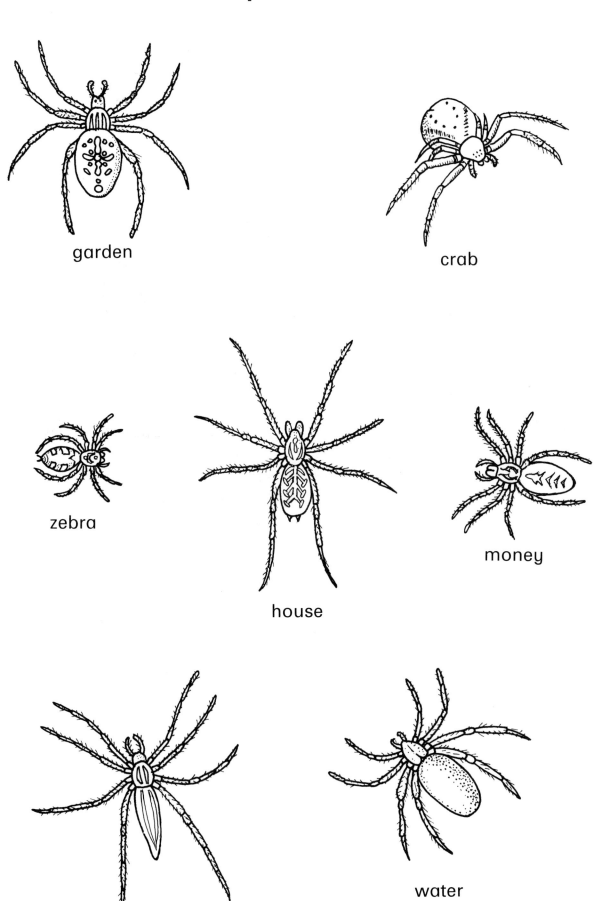

garden

crab

zebra

house

money

wolf

water

Red-kneed tarantula

Spiderword

Clues down
1. Striped animal spider?
3. Variety sharing your home
4. Fast-running brown spider
5. 12 mm long and dangerous

Clues across
2. Cob web to catch insects
6. Sideways walking spider
7. Spiders' food
8. Spins tube-shaped web in cracks
9. Spiders have eight

Spiders 6

Caught by spider

Start

Finish

SIGNS

Science

- Signs of animals and birds
- Recording 'invisible' creatures
- Signs of invertebrate life

Geography

- Neighbourhood signs
- Sign recording and classification
- Signs of the road
- The Highway Code – legal signs
- Suggestions for new signs
- Warning signs
- Signs of changing weather
- Weather forecasting signs
- Signs as symbols: use of keys
- Inn signs
- Signposts

Mathematics

- Graphing birth signs
- Signing in numbers for the deaf

SIGNS

History

- Medieval signs
- Heraldry
- Runes – magical signs
- Famous signs

Health Education

- Signs of ill-health
- Symptoms for action

English

- 'Sign' – its various meanings
- The power of signs
- Advertising signs
- Body language 'signs'
- 'Sign word' stories
- Sign sayings
- Signatures
- Sign language for the deaf
- Semaphore
- Star signs and fortune telling

Music

- Songs and music about signs

Art

- Visual qualities of signs
- Design of advertisements
- Casts of animal and bird tracks
- Coats of arms and heraldic devices
- Family coat of arms
- Signs of the zodiac wall hangings

BASIC CONCEPTS

1 We use signs and symbols every day for a variety of purposes.

2 Signs can give warnings, information, evidence, and can be used for communication.

3 Signs can be tangible objects – signboards, etc. – or they can be indicators of feelings and events.

STARTING POINTS

• Take a walk into the neighbourhood and make general observations of signs and symbols, including road and traffic signs, business and commercial signs, pub signs, etc.

• Collect literature on published signs, for example, the Highway Code.

• Learn some signs that can be used for communication, for example, semaphore or sign language for the deaf.

• Look up the word 'sign' in dictionaries and discuss its various meanings. Pursue these in various phases and emphases of the topic.

GEOGRAPHY

Activity 1: Signs and symbols in the street

• Take the class out into the local area, through town streets if possible, and make general observations of the signs and symbols to be found there. Discuss findings and help children to appreciate the wide range of signs we find all around us in everyday life – road and traffic signs, commercial and business signs (shops, banks,

building societies), pub signs, general information signs, advertising billboards and posters, and so on. As a result of these general observations, group the signs observed under the following headings, and let the children draw or paint examples from each category. The categories suggested below can, of course, be added to or changed.

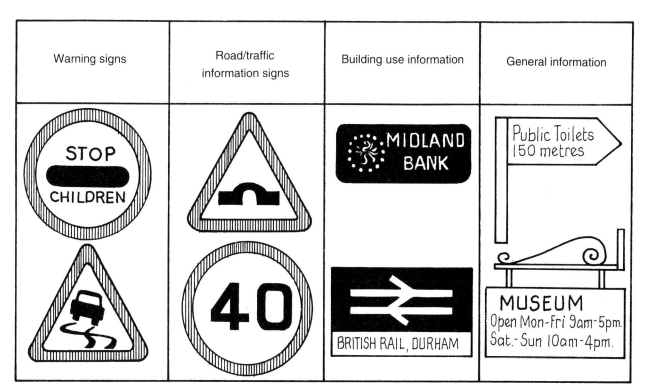

Warning signs	Road/traffic information signs	Building use information	General information

Some familiar signs

● Make a more detailed study of signs in the locality by systematic recording, description and analysis. Perhaps the children could be divided into groups, and each group asked to focus on a particular type of sign. For example, one group could concentrate on banks and building societies, one on advertising signs, one on general information signs, and so on. In the field, the children should sketch each sign, note its colours so that it can be painted later, and describe what it shows. Back in the classroom, suggest that each sign is painted and accompanied by a detailed description, together with a statement about why the sign is needed, what it tells people and (if relevant) why people would visit the place advertised by the sign. For example:

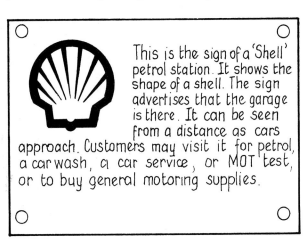

This is the sign of a 'Shell' petrol station. It shows the shape of a shell. The sign advertises that the garage is there. It can be seen from a distance as cars approach. Customers may visit it for petrol, a car wash, a car service, or MOT test, or to buy general motoring supplies.

● Display the results of the above activity, thus building up a comprehensive set of analyses of all the signs in the neighbourhood. If you are visiting a busy town centre, then clearly the area studied will need to be restricted, otherwise the number of signs could easily run into hundreds! Be sure to make children aware of the importance of road safety at all times.

Activity 2: Traffic signs
● Focus on traffic signs. As well as observing those in the immediate locality, provide copies of the Highway Code for the children to use for research. Use **Copymaster 1** as a basis for this work. The Copymaster shows 12 road and traffic signs, taken from the Highway Code. First of all, have a class quiz to see how many of these signs the children can identify, before looking up the correct answers. Then use the Highway Code to ascertain the correct interpretation of each sign. Let the children colour the signs, pointing out to them the significance of ensuring that the colours are accurate.

Activity 3: The Highway Code
● Follow on from the above activity by discussing the status of the Highway Code. This is a legally binding document. Try to find out what the penalties might be for motorists and other road users who do not observe the rules and signs of the Code. Discuss why we need a set of rules and road signs at all, and consider their various categories: for example, warning signs, information signs, speed restrictions, etc. Note the significance of colour and shape in the grouping of various kinds of road signs.

● Consider inviting an officer from your local police station to come and talk to the children about road signs in the area. If this can be arranged, give the officer a specific brief – for example, he or she could comment on whether there are any new signs or traffic lights, and if so why they were put there (because of requests from local residents, because the site is known as a recognised 'accident black spot', etc.). Another line of discussion could be on the penalties for ignoring or disobeying signs, and why the police force must take adherence to the Highway Code very seriously.

● Ask the children to assess the local neighbourhood themselves, and decide whether they think any further signs (of any kind) would be useful or helpful. Perhaps they could design new signs, if appropriate. Suggestions could be forwarded to the police or town planning office if they have the genuine potential to improve the neighbourhood or to make it safer – a useful letter-writing exercise.

Activity 4: Warning signs
● Focus on warning signs. As a result of fieldwork and research in books and magazines, make a class collection of drawings of 'signs that warn us'. See if these signs have anything in common; perhaps large, clear lettering or bright colours. Discuss the need for such signs to be clearly visible, perhaps from a distance (relate to Art activities 19 and 20).

Activity 5: Weather signs
● Investigate 'signs' that help to tell us about the weather and its changing patterns. This could well be linked to Science activities on measuring and forecasting aspects of the weather. Ask children to observe the weather and related elements such as the sky, the air and the ground over a period of time, and to design posters that show how 'signs', in the sense of observed phenomena, can help us as amateur weather forecasters. Such signs might include:

Red sky at night ...... leads to a fine day.

Tall heavy black clouds ...lead to thunderstorms.

Clear, cold winter night .... heavy frost by morning.

Heavy, whitish-grey clouds in winter.... perhaps a snowstorm.

Weather signs

● Make a study of signs (in the sense of symbols) used by weather forecasters on television. This activity could be started by asking the children to watch the television weather forecasts (or bringing into the classroom a videotape recording of, say, the previous evening's forecast for today). Ask them to observe any signs used, then make their own weather maps for display in school, so that other children in the school will know what the weather is likely to be. A new map could be drawn each day, or you could make a base map with movable symbols that can be altered each day. Again, this activity has clear links with science, as the children will ideally need to have a knowledge of aspects of the weather and its vocabulary, such as 'depressions' and 'cold fronts', in order to fully comprehend the signs. Perhaps a classroom display of familiar TV weather signs could be made:

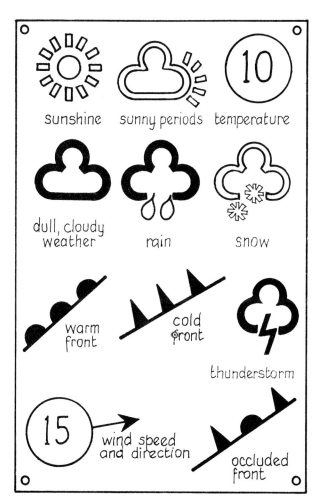

Weather chart symbols

● Link the above activity with development of, for example, geographical concepts of the use of symbols and keys. Let the children discuss whether they think television weather symbols are appropriate and easily understood. Could they design others? Make a set of original symbols for use on classroom weather charts, helping the children to appreciate that the whole point of signs as symbols is that other people can easily interpret them.

Activity 6: Tavern signs
● Make a special study of inn, public house and hotel signs. This could be done in your area, and the children could 'I-Spy' them when travelling. Use **Copymaster 2** to introduce this interesting subject. Begin by studying each sign spotted. What does it mean? Does it commemorate a legend, a famous person or event, a local custom or a mythological character? Is the design painted on a flat board, or does it project out into the street? Sketch or photograph the sign, if possible. Look out for any indication of the age of the inn.

Background information
In medieval times, when few people could read, each trade or merchant guild had a symbol by which its product or service could be identified. A statute of King Richard II which was enacted in 1393 required brewers to identify houses in which ale was sold, hence the proliferation of tavern and inn signs after that time. Originally, the sign was intended to help the King's ale taster to plan his sampling visits, rather than to attract custom from the general public.

Inn signs can be classified in various ways. Perhaps the following groupings will be useful should the children wish to specialise in studying particular types of signs.

– **Royal:** The Monarch, The Crown, The Rose, The Queen Victoria, The Rose and Crown (commemorating the marriage of Henry Tudor and Elizabeth of York), The Prince Rupert, The Prince of Wales, The Royal George (which one?), The Royal Oak (connections here with the escape of Charles II by hiding in an oak tree), The King's Head (which King?), The King Edward VII, and so on.
– **Baronial:** The Swan (The Duke of Buckingham), The Boar (Lancaster), The Bear and Ragged Staff (Warwick), The Duke of Clarence, The Duke of Edinburgh, The Duke of York, amongst others.
– **People:** including Adam and Eve, Admiral Nelson, Dick Turpin, Florence Nightingale, King Charles II, Amy Johnson, Napoleon, James Brindley, Ben Jonson, Lord Byron, Oliver Cromwell, Shakespeare, Wellington, and many more.
– **Mythological:** The Unicorn, The Minotaur, The Mermaid, The Angel, The George and Dragon, The Firebird, The Green Man (connections with the story of John Barleycorn), etc.
– **Events:** (presumably commemorating the battles of) Waterloo, Trafalgar, etc.
– **Animals and birds:** The Eagle, The Red Lion, The Tiger's Head, The Porcupine, The Antelope, The Hen and Chickens, The Black (or White) Horse, The Cheshire Cat (from which famous story?), The Cock and Magpie, The Duck, The Fox and Goose, The Frighted Horse (scope for creative writing here?), The Lion and Lamb, The Lazy Fox, The Pelican, The Pig and Whistle, The Stag, The Stork, The Squirrel, The Wren's Nest, and so on.
– **Sports and pastimes:** The Fisherman, The Cricketer's Arms, The Bear (bear baiting), The Dog and Pheasant/Partridge (shooting), The Winning Post (racing), The Jolly Huntsman (hunting), The Harriers, The Sportsman, The Stirrup Cup, etc.

– **Occupations:** The Plough (farmers), The Wheatsheaf (corn-chandlers), The Golden Fleece, The Woolpack (wool merchants), The Beehive, The Blacksmith's Arms, The Gunmaker's Arms, The Jeweller's Arms, The Lamplighter, The Long Boat (canals), The Old Smithy, The Pen and Wig (legal profession?), The Woodman (forestry), The Town Crier, The Bottle And Glass (glass-blowing), The Chainmaker's Arms, and so on.

– **Curiosities:** The World Turned Upside Down, The Cauliflower Ear (probably from the pastime of boxing!), The Old Contemptibles, The Barrel Organ, The Foaming Tankard, The Ring O' Bells, The Sacks of Potatoes, The Slug and Lettuce, The Unspoilt By Progress, The Yard of Ale, etc.

Inn signs which commemorate travel can be a separate study on their own, covering modes of transport from medieval times to the present day. This could include:

– **the age of pilgrimage,** when religious foundations cared for travellers. Look for names like The Bull (from 'bulla', a monastic seal), The Cross Keys (often near a church dedicated to St. Peter), The Compasses (from the saying 'God encompasseth us'), pubs named after saints or Bible characters, or historical events (The Turk's Head or The Crusader).

– **The age of wool,** with names like The Pack Horse, The Jolly Carter, The Woolpack, The Golden Fleece, The Waggoner's Rest, The Flock and The Shepherd. Signs like these were often found along the main cross-country routes used by waggoners taking wool and cloth to the great ports of medieval England.

– **the age of coaches and coaching inns,** with names like The Turnpike, The Tollgate, The Coach and Horses, The Royal Mail, The Groom, Halfway House, and so on.

– **the ages of various types of transport,** such as sail (The Cutty Sark, The Jolly Sailors, The Safe Harbour, The Man O' War), steam (The Great Western, The Iron Horse, The Railway Arms, The Rocket, The George Stephenson, The Locomotive), and so on.

● The children could either design and colour an imaginary sign on the inn in the Copymaster picture, or reproduce a field sketch of a genuine sign. Discuss the origin of inn and public house signs, and of course their related names. Some have fascinating histories, and local guidebooks may well explain the significance of a particular hostelry's name. Make a book of interesting local pub signs, with pictures and stories of their origins or connections. A collection of paintings of interesting inn signs would make an eye-catching wall display, especially with written interpretations of their significance.

● In the case of names like 'The Slug And Lettuce', a more light-hearted 'spare time' activity would be to invent some more unusual 'pub pairs' and draw appropriate signs for them. What might the signs for 'The Owl And Pussy Cat' or 'The Frog and Nightgown' look like? What is the most 'peculiar pub' name they can devise – and could the children write a story to explain how this name came about?

Activity 7: Historical signs

● How do we learn about ancient history? What signs have our ancestors left behind? Tell the children about the work of an archaeologist, and take them to a museum to view the results of the archaeologist's work. Ask the children to sketch some of the exhibits, and make a list of all the different 'signs' that tell us about our past. Perhaps they could write a story about how they discovered one such historical sign.

● Tell the children about, or let them research, the runic signs used by the Vikings. (Link with activities suggested in the **Blueprints** *History Key Stage 2 Teacher's Resource Book*.) Let the children create their own messages or secret signs. Explain the magical significance of runes to the Vikings.

● Ask the children to research where our written number signs came from. Contrast our system with others, such as Roman numerals. Can the children invent a new set of signs for numerals?

● A similar activity could be undertaken with ancient alphabets, such as the Greek, Roman or Egyptian.

● Let the children speculate on what a medieval street or marketplace would have looked like. Remembering that few people could read in those days, the tradesmen (apothecaries, knifegrinders, carpenters, butchers, drapers, etc.) would each need a clear sign by which customers could recognise their wares. Create a bustling medieval street scene, with lots of shoppers browsing amidst many colourful stalls and signs. There will probably be enough ancient trades to enable each child to contribute a sign for this frieze.

Activity 8: Road signposts

● Look at road signposts – in the locality, if possible. Also, ask the children to look out for signposts when travelling away from home. Discuss the qualities of a good signpost: presumably clarity of information, legibility from a distance and sensible siting. Ask the children to evaluate signposts in your home area – are they serving the purpose for which they are intended?

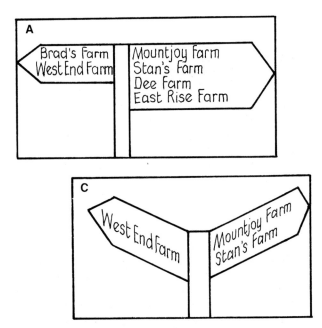

Possible solutions to Copymaster 3

Can the children suggest designs for new signs? Are there road junctions not currently signposted where signs would be very helpful?

Use **Copymaster 3** to help the children think through the complexities of signposting an area. This shows an imaginary village area, with six farms, and six road junctions. When approaching from the Hallgarth road, a traveller who does not know the area would no doubt have considerable difficulty in accurately locating one or more of the farms without efficient signposts. Let the children study the map on the Copymaster, then, in the boxes in the lower half of the sheet, draw accurate signposts that should be in place at each of the junctions, labelled A–F. An example of this is shown on the previous page.

This activity is more complex than it may appear at first sight!

HEALTH EDUCATION

Activity 9: Signs as symptoms
• Discuss how 'signs' can be used to indicate whether we are healthy or not. In health terms, we usually use the word 'symptoms' as signs or indicators of ill-health. Let the children suggest common signs of ailments, such as raised body temperature, stomach ache, skin rash, etc.
• Pursue this theme by making a more systematic list or dictionary of 'health signs'. Children could list symptoms and, after discussion or further research, add suggestions for action at the appearance of each sign.

Note: this activity could well be undertaken in consultation with the school nurse, in order to ensure accuracy of information and advice. Children should appreciate that all 'signs' or symptoms should be treated seriously – and whilst it is not appropriate to call the doctor for every spot or sneeze, we should always be on the alert for possible signs of serious ill-health, and seek medical attention whenever appropriate.

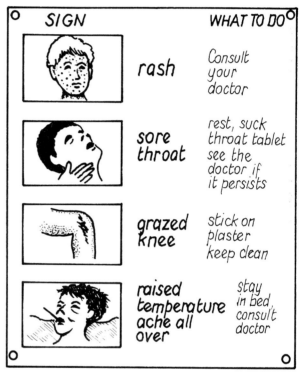

Health signs

SCIENCE

Activity 10: Signs in the animal kingdom
• Investigate signs in the animal kingdom, in the sense of indications that an animal, bird or insect is or has been present. Take the children out on field visits, to explore and record evidence in the form of tracks and other signs. A winter's day when the ground is snowy or frosty is an ideal time to hunt for bird or mammal tracks, and a variety of other signs of life can be observed at all times of the year.

Copymaster 4 suggests possible signs to look for, and provides a recording sheet which can be taken into the field. Children should hunt carefully for evidence and write the date on which the sign(s) were discovered in the appropriate column, together with an identification of the creature which might have made the sign, and a field sketch. For example:

| Animal tracks | 16.4. | rabbit |
| Bird pellets | 28.6. | barn owl |

85

● After several field observations of the above kind, suggest that the children write accounts of 'the invisible animals', telling of the range of wildlife that has obviously visited or lives in a particular habitat (woodland, field, hedgerow, etc.), and of the sign evidence that has been left behind. Encourage observation of signs that may not be included on the Copymaster – for example, moved earth, or holes in the ground whose originator may not easily be identified.

● Design a similar recording sheet for signs of invertebrate activity. Let the children make suggestions for this sheet. Precise identification of the absent insect or other invertebrate may, of course, be very difficult, but encouraging children to look for signs will assist the development of close observation skills. How easy it is to walk past a tree and not notice holes in its leaves .... Suggestions for observing and recording may include the following, but do encourage spontaneous 'I-Spy' in the field.

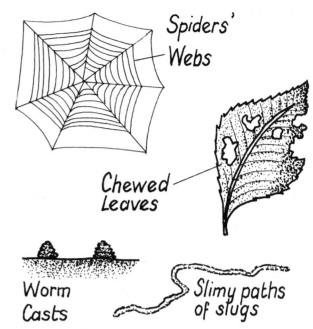

Look out for signs of invertebrate life too

ENGLISH

Activity 11: What does the word 'sign' mean?
● Discuss the meaning of the word 'sign', and ask the children to look it up in a number of dictionaries. They will see that it has a variety of meanings: for example, one dictionary says that a sign is a 'thing indicative or suggestive of quality or state' (e.g. a sign of weakness) or a 'thing perceived as indicating future state or occurrence' (e.g. the first signs of spring). A sign can also be a symbol ...a word ...a gesture ...a sound ...or a signboard. It can be used in the sense of 'to sign one's name'. Talk about the many ways we use the word in everyday language, and define the parameters of your topic. Help children to appreciate that in the topic as a whole, the word will be employed in a number of different ways.

Activity 12: The power of signs
● Talk about the concept of 'the power of signs'. Look at tourist brochures promoting city life. It is highly likely that they will include photographs of the city at night, with neon signs and brightly lit advertisements adorning the buildings. Discuss the power of signs to advertise, and consider the qualities of advertisement signs which attract people – presumably their brightness, visual impact, colour scheme, vibrant message, humour or perhaps a combination of these factors (link with Art activities). See how many advertising slogans have impressed themselves upon the children's consciousness through TV commercials, etc.

Background information
One of the most powerful of all signs was that of Lord Kitchener's 'Your Country Needs You' recruiting poster in 1914, which resulted in many thousands of patriotic Englishmen joining up to fight in France.

A famous sign – the Lord Kitchener recruiting poster, displayed in the early days of the Great War (1914). Why was it so successful?

● Ask the children to select their favourite signboard advertisement – from magazines, tourist brochures or real life – and to explain why they have chosen it. Compare the explanations of various children in the class, and see if a consensus of criteria for 'visual impact' emerges.

● Discuss the use of the word 'sign' as relating to indicating feelings or behaviour. Link this to signs revealed by body language – for example, discuss what is meant by 'showing signs of weakness', 'showing signs of stress', displaying all the 'signs of success'. Perhaps this activity could be developed into role play situations, in which children act out these signs, with appropriate body and possibly spoken language.

Activity 13: Stories about signs
● Suggest that the children write stories incorporating signs (i.e. signboards) instead of words wherever possible. For example:

Last Saturday I set out to **C&A** to buy some new slippers. It took me ages to get there on my bicycle. Every set of 🚦 was on red. Eventually, I arrived. 🚦 Then I discovered I did not have enough money. Oh, dear, off to **BARCLAYS** bank. On the way back from the bank, I stopped off at **Boots** and guess what I bought...

Activity 14: Sayings about signs
● Think of common sayings involving the word 'sign', and discuss their meanings. For example, 'a sign of the times', 'the first signs of spring', and so on. Each could be the focus of poster-style illustrations, conveying images created by the use of the word 'sign' in each case.

Activity 15: Personal signs
● Ask the children how they can make their personal 'signs'. The answer is, of course, with their signatures or 'signing' of their identity. Enhance any display relating to the topic of 'signs' with a border of the children's own signatures. If these are done in paint and brushwork, they may not be as neat as when done with a finer instrument, but will form an interesting and clearly visible aspect of your display.

Activity 16: Signs for the hard of hearing
● Help the children to appreciate how vitally important signs are to the deaf and hard of hearing. This is a splendid lead in to the importance of signs for non-verbal communication, highlighted in both Copymasters 5 and 6.

Begin with **Copymaster 5**. This is the finger spelling alphabet of the Royal National Institute for the Deaf. Children can work in pairs to learn this alphabet, and to practise communicating with it. This activity could lead in to a study of other signing systems used with the deaf and hard of hearing, such as Makaton.

Background information
Further information may be obtained from:

The Royal National Institute for the Deaf
105 Gower Street
London
WC1E 6AH

The Beverley School for the Deaf, Middlesbrough has produced an extensive and illustrated signing dictionary, *Communication Link*, which was sponsored by Cleveland County Council Education Department, and first published in 1986. This book would be extremely valuable to anyone interested in learning more about signing for the deaf. All enquiries should be addressed to:

Beverley School for the Deaf
Beverley Road
Saltersgill
Middlesbrough
Cleveland
TS4 3QL

● Provide the children with a sheet showing the signs for the numbers 1–10 as used when signing with the deaf, similar to the one below:

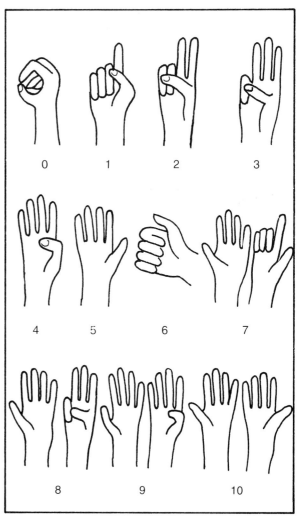

How to sign in numbers (Source: RNID)

Use it to set simple mathematical questions and ask the children to 'sign' their answers rather than writing them down.

Activity 17: Visual signing

● Continue studies of non-verbal communication by suggesting that the children learn the flag language of semaphore. Use **Copymaster 6** to teach this. Ideally, you will need several pairs of flags, so that the children can practise sending and receiving messages in pairs. These flags can easily be made by sewing squares of material onto lengths of dowel. Teach the message 'start' sign first, i.e. both flags dipped in front of the sender, then the letters of the alphabet. Simple messages can be exchanged by pairs of children standing at opposite ends of the school hall or playground. Note that if an error is made, they should signal the sign for the letter 'E' eight times.

Activity 18: Star signs

● Pursue the subject of 'star signs', with **Copymaster 7**. Here is an opportunity to link this overall topic with scientific information about constellations of stars, and this Copymaster could well be used alongside Copymaster 6 and related activities of the Space topic, p. 143. In the present Copymaster 7, we are shown an artist's creative impression of the 12 signs of the zodiac, together with their associated birth dates. Let each child identify his or her own birth sign. Discuss why we use such expressions as 'star signs' and 'signs of the zodiac'.

Ask the children to research the significance or meanings of the various signs of the zodiac. Designs for these signs would make colourful embroidered or collage wall hangings for the classroom walls.

A worthwhile mathematical exercise would be to graph the number of children within the class who are Taureans, Sagittarians, etc., and display the results. This could be extended to include every class and the staff in the school. Which sign of the zodiac dominates your school (in terms of numbers of pupils and staff)?

You may not wish to pass judgement on the validity or otherwise of horoscopes, but the children will no doubt be aware of the fact that 'fortunes in the stars' are regularly printed in newspapers and magazines. Let the children read their own star sign fortunes over a period of time, and discuss whether these predictions seem to have any bearing on reality. If you wish to pursue this subject further, specialist books on the zodiac signs could be consulted (readily available in popular newsagents and libraries), and the children could research the alleged personality characteristics belonging to people of each birth sign of the zodiac.

Note: this activity should be treated with sensitivity. Some parents may not wish their children to engage in astrology and fortune telling, whilst others may take star signs and predictions of future events very seriously. Use it as an opportunity to discuss the fact that there are sensitive issues in life about which opinions vary, and that we should respect the personal views of others.

ART

Activity 19: What makes a 'good' sign?

● Discuss the qualities of 'good' signs, which will of course depend on what the signs are intending to convey – information, advertising messages, warnings or whatever. Let the children design and paint examples of successful signs in each category. Aspects that must be considered are as follows:

- colour (strength, combination)
- lettering (size, spacing, colour)
- shape
- size
- general visual impact
- design
- background
- main features.

Activity 20: Design a sign

● Perhaps competitions could be organised to see who could design and paint the most eye-catching advertisement, the best information sign, the most effective warning sign, etc. (Link with Activity 20 in the Colour topic, p. 106, on the need to select the colour of lettering so that it is visible from a distance.)

● Turn one of your classroom frieze boards into an advertising sign board: let the class co-operate in the design and creation of a huge advertising feature for a chosen product or commodity. Perhaps the children could vote on suggestions for such a product before designs are submitted; alternatively, a more adventurous and creative approach might be to invent a new product for which an appropriate advertising campaign must be planned. What sign(s) can the children create for

- a new hair preparation
- a new pet food
- a new sweet or snack food
- a new cleaning product
- a new form of transport
and so on....

● On a more light-hearted note, the children could design a 'Wanted' poster similar to those seen in cowboy films, bearing a portrait (of themselves?) and details of the crime(s) they have committed. And don't forget the reward!

• Perhaps the children can design signs to help visitors find their way around the school, or labels for classrooms, wall displays, and the like.

Activity 21: Capture a sign
• Make casts of animal and/or bird signs, such as footprints or tracks.

You will need:
plaster of Paris
water
a disposable paper cup
a strip of thick card 6 cm deep
a paperclip.

What to do:
Place the card in a circular band around the track and fasten it with the paperclip. Mix the plaster of Paris with water in the disposable container until it reaches a suitable consistency, and pour it into the circle containing the print or track. Wait for it to set. Pick up the cast carefully and take it back to the classroom. Brush off any loose soil. After a few days, remove the card ring before painting and/or varnishing the animal sign.

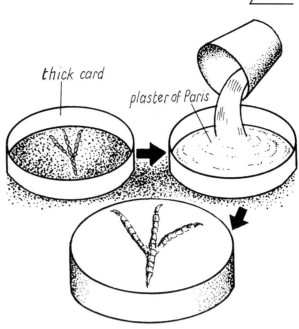

Making a cast of a sign in the field

Activity 22: Heraldic signs
• Ask the children how the soldiers in a medieval army could distinguish friend from foe, particularly if they were encased in a heavy suit of armour. The answer, of course, lay in coats of arms or heraldic signs which identified each knight's company of soldiers.

How could you tell friend from foe in a battle like this one?

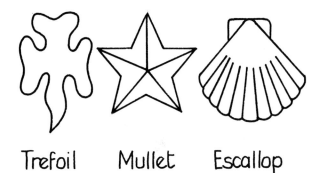

Trefoil   Mullet   Escallop

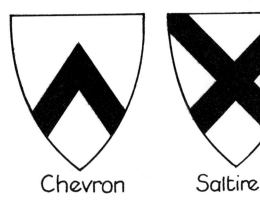

Chevron   Saltire

Some symbols used in heraldry

• Children could research the art of heraldry in reference books and paint banners or shields in particularly prominent or attractive designs.
• Challenge the children to create their own family coat of arms. The design should be connected in some way with the family name, tradition or occupation wherever possible – perhaps arrows for the Fletcher family, anvils for the Smiths, cottage loaves for the Bakers, a sword or dagger for the Steel(e) family, and so on. Some of these may seem a little contrived, but hopefully most children will be able to devise a suitable 'image' of this kind without undue difficulty.

Background information
The earliest coats of arms were very simple – perhaps a cross or a bar, or a brightly coloured creature (usually looking very fierce). As more and more noblemen created their own coats of arms, the designs became more complicated in order to avoid copying existing ones. The College of Arms was established in 1484 to regulate the creation of coats of arms and heraldic devices, and it still exists to this day.

• Does the school have a badge or a coat of arms? If so, try to discover its meaning. If not, ask the children to design a suitable one.

MUSIC

Activity 23: Music about signs
• Suggestions for appropriate music connected with signs to which the children could listen include 'Aquarius/Let The Sunshine' from the musical *Hair*, and the instrumental 'At The Sign Of The Swinging Cymbal' which was disc jockey Alan Freeman's signature tune on BBC Radio 1 for many years.

Village inn

Signposts

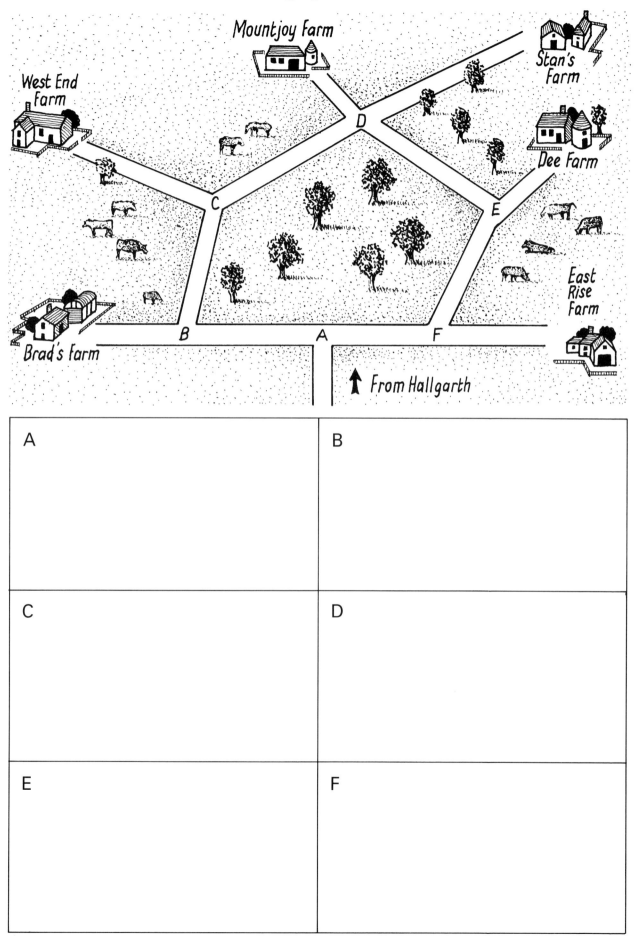

A	B
C	D
E	F

 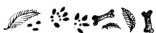 # Signs of animals and birds

SIGN	DATE	IDENTIFICATION
Birds' nests		
Bird pellets		
Bird tracks		
Bird droppings		
Feathers		
Animal homes		
Mammal bones		
Meal remains		
Chewed cones or nuts		
Animal tracks		
Animal droppings		
Fur or wool		

Spelling with signs

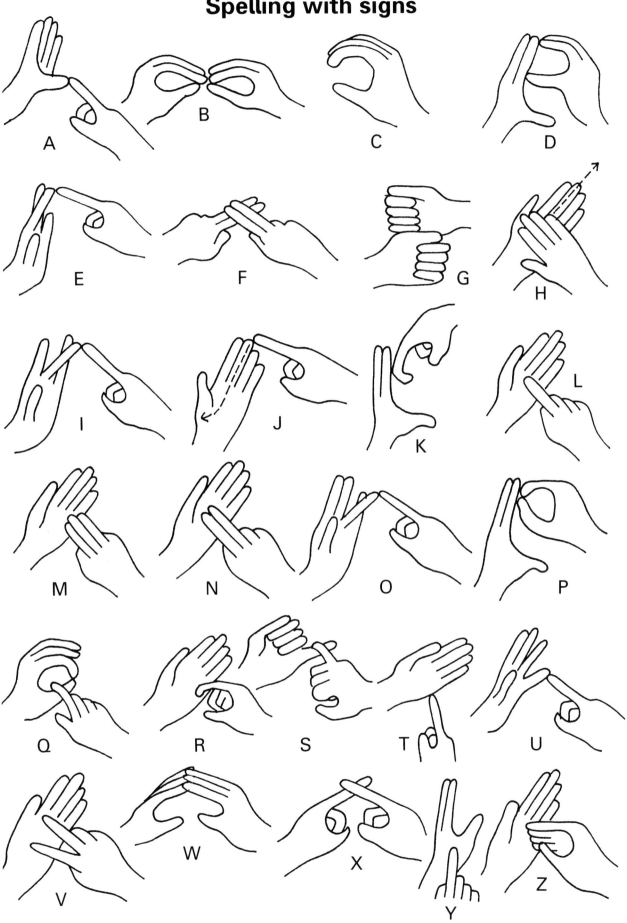

Semaphore

Start

A B C

D E F G H

I J K L M

N O P Q R

S T U V W

X Y Z

If you make a mistake, signal E eight times

☆ ☆ ☆ ☆☆☆ **Fortunes in the stars** ☆☆ ☆ ☆ ☆ ☆ ☆

Aries	Taurus	Gemini
(Mar 21–Apr 20)	(Apr 21–May 21)	(May 22–Jun 21)
Cancer	Leo	Virgo
(Jun 22–Jul 23)	(Jul 24–Aug 23)	(Aug 24–Sep 23)
Libra	Scorpio	Sagittarius
(Sep 24–Oct 23)	(Oct 24–Nov 22)	(Nov 23–Dec 21)
Capricorn	Aquarius	Pisces
(Dec 22–Jan 20)	(Jan 21–Feb 19)	(Feb 20–Mar 20)

COLOUR

Science
- Observe or make a rainbow
- Splitting of white light
- Colour wheels
- Using colour filters
- Filter spectacles
- Colour box
- 'Changing' colour: how we see
- Mixing coloured lights
- Plant colours: chlorophyll
- Common flower colours
- Animal colouring – camouflage
- Animals which change colour
- Colours of the sky
- Sunrise and sunset
- Colours of the TV screen
- Computerised colours

Art
- Interior design – mixing and matching colour
- 'Feel' of home colours
- Decorated colour wheels
- Shades of a single colour
- Mixing paint colours
- Primary colours of light and paint
- Animal camouflage colours
- Sunrise and sunset colours
- Power of colour – in advertising and signs
- Make natural dyes
- Tie and dye
- Chromatography patterns
- Marbling
- Stained glass windows

History
- Sir Isaac Newton: the Newtonian colour disc

COLOUR

Geography/Mathematics
- Neighbourhood colour surveys – cars and front door colours
- Human skin colours
- Colour for identity: eyes and hair
- Mathematical rainbows

English
- Rainbow colours – favourite colours
- Worlds of a single colour
- Moods of colour
- Subtle shades of colour
- Paint colour names
- Tastes of colour
- Colour poems
- Deprived of colour
- Colour in words, phrases and sayings
- Colour songs

Health Education
- How we see colour
- Colour blindness
- Animal eyesight

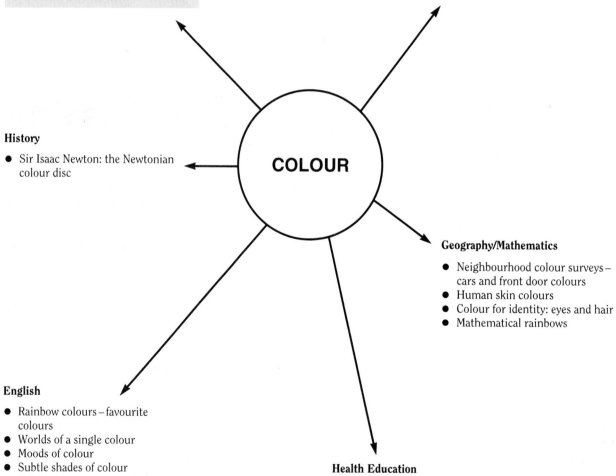

BASIC CONCEPTS

1 Colours enhance our world and give our surroundings interest. Some colours may please us, others we may not enjoy so much. Most people have favourite colours.

2 White light is a spectrum, made up of seven main colours. Three of these – red, blue and green – are the primary colours of light.

3 Mixing paints can result in the production of an almost limitless number of subtle shades. The three primary colours of paints are red, blue and yellow.

4 Human beings rely to an extent on colour for their identity. Each of us has our own particular colour of skin, eyes and hair.

5 Colours are also important in the worlds of animals and plants.

STARTING POINTS

● Go around the class asking each person to name their favourite colour. See if a class 'favourite' emerges, and discuss why individuals like it.

● Observe a rainbow … or make one.

● Go on a 'colour walk' in the school grounds or neighbourhood, to look for the incidence of colour in the natural and built environments.

● Acquire some paint sample charts, showing the wide range of colours available and the names that have been given to them.

● Mix paints: see how many colours can be made.

ENGLISH

 C1–2

Activity 1: Favourite colours

● Use **Copymaster 1** as a starting point for helping the children to think about the role and importance of colour in the world. First, this Copymaster provides an opportunity for reminding children of the accepted colours of the rainbow and the order in which these occur: red, orange, yellow, green, blue, indigo, violet. This provides an early link in the topic between science and creative activities. Second, it provides an opportunity for the children to think about colours and to record which is their favourite. Ask them to colour the rainbow in its correct colours, then to reflect on which of these is their favourite, and to draw and colour as many things as possible of the chosen colour in the space below.

Decisions will have to be made about whether the children's choice is restricted to rainbow colours, or whether the rules will be 'bent' to allow, for example, favourite shades of colour such as pink, grey and white to be chosen. An advantage of staying with the rainbow colours is that this activity can then easily be linked with mathematics. The number of 'votes' for each of the seven colours can be worked out, and block graphs drawn to show the favourite colours of the class. One purpose of this Copymaster is to help children think through the incidence of one of the colours in the world – how and where it occurs naturally and in man-made objects in their lives.

● When each child has completed this Copymaster, go around the class and ask each person to hold up their sheet, so that others can see the chosen colour, reflected in the items drawn. Ask each person to talk about why they have chosen that colour – to put into words what is special about it. Discuss the children's comments. Ask, for example, whether they would like it if everything in the world was of their favourite colour … would they like, for example, all their food to be blue or violet … would they get bored if every item of clothing was red … what would a world of yellow trees, grass and sea be like … ?

● Following on from the above activity, suggest that the children write poems and imaginative stories about 'A Blue World', 'The Day The World Went Red' and so on, telling of what the consequences were for animal, plant and human life.

● Tell the story of Joseph and his coat of many colours, or perhaps arrange a visit to a performance of the Andrew Lloyd Webber/Tim Rice production of *Joseph and the Amazing Technicolor Dreamcoat*. Perhaps the children could paint pictures of what they think Joseph's coat looked like.

Activity 2: The 'moods' of colour

● **Copymaster 2** provides a recording sheet for an extension of work on thinking about the enjoyment, 'moods' and 'emotions' of colour. This is essentially an individual activity in the first instance. Ask each child to sit quietly and think about the 'moods' of different colours, how colours make them feel. They should then be asked to look at the words under the frames – 'happy', 'sad', 'hot', 'cold', etc., and to try to associate a colour with each of these feelings. A picture should be drawn in each frame to represent the feeling, and it should be coloured in the colour which first came to mind when thinking about its title. When each child has completed his/her picture, share results around the class. See to what extent there is a consensus (perhaps red/orange for hot, etc.) and discuss why this may be so. See where major variations in interpretations through colour occur.

Activity 3: Colour charts
● Collect some paint sample charts and let the children study them. Discuss the great range of colours and subtle shades that is available. Suggest that each child selects colours that they would like to have in the school/classroom/home (link with art activities).
● Read the names given to colours on paint charts; exchange opinions on which names are appropriate. Which are most likely to attract people to buy the paint? Let the children draw and colour in their own chart and make up original names for the colours they show on it.

Activity 4: The taste of colour
● Write poems and imaginative prose about 'the wonderful taste of colour', reflecting on coloured foods and drinks that have a particularly good taste. This could of course be linked to scientific investigations into food colourings and the link between colour and flavour. For example, test to see whether children can identify the colours of Smarties when blindfolded, merely by their taste.

Activity 5: Writing about colour
● Write colour poems, with a particular colour as a theme, for example, 'The Richness of Red', 'The Dull Grey Morning', 'All Things Blue And Beautiful', etc.
● Ask the children to write imaginative stories about what it would be like suddenly to be deprived of colour vision. How would the world appear? What would be the many difficulties they would encounter in going about their everyday lives?
● Expand on this activity by asking the children to think of occasions when colour is important to us – for example, traffic lights helping with road safety, pillar boxes for our letters, colours to distinguish different sports teams and so on. Which coloured flags suggest surrender and danger? What is the 'chequered flag' used for?
● How many proverbs, sayings and expressions can the children collect about colours? Here are some to begin with:

– 'Every cloud has a silver lining.'
– 'The pot calling the kettle black.'
– 'Silence is golden.'
– 'There it is, in black and white.'
– 'He was the black sheep of the family.'

– 'He had blue blood in his veins.'
– 'It was a red letter day for me.'
– 'The pages of the book were yellow with age.'
– 'My bank account has gone into the red.'
as well as:
– 'blue with cold', 'purple with rage', 'green with envy', 'white with fear', 'blood-red', 'bottle-green', 'brick-red', 'coal-black', 'nut-brown', 'pea-green', 'shell-pink', 'slate-grey', 'canary-yellow', 'as brown as a berry', 'as purple as the heather', 'as black as pitch', 'silver-tongued' and so on.

Ask the children to explain what these sayings mean, and/or how they might have come about. What happens when we see someone 'in their true colours'?

Activity 6: Colour vocabulary
● Linking with the previous activity, start individual or class books about colour. Include as many shades of colour as possible, together with as many 'colour' words as the children can find. These might include:
cherry, jet, maroon, emerald, violet, tangerine, carmine, vermilion, turquoise, scarlet, auburn, tan, golden, ruby, inky, buff, russet, flaxen, primrose, sooty, murky, tawny, ebony, lemon, peach, azure, puce, ivory, crimson, bronze; and also words such as pigment, tint, shade, pale, vivid, garish, luminous, translucent, pallid, opaque, spectrum, etc.

Activity 7: Songs of colour
● Find (and sing) as many songs about colour as you and the children can discover. Start with 'I Can Sing A Rainbow', 'Yellow Submarine' and 'Lavender Blue' … how many more can you find?
Extend this activity to a competition to see how many song or instrumental music titles the children can find which have a colour in them. This makes a useful 'spare time' activity. However, if parents and friends are involved, the results may well be quite surprising! Here are some suggestions with which to begin the list:
'The White Cliffs of Dover', 'Bye Bye, Blackbird', 'Blue Moon', 'Red Sails In The Sunset', 'Singing The Blues', 'The Green, Green Grass Of Home', 'Green Door', 'Paint It Black', 'Tie A Yellow Ribbon', 'A Whiter Shade Of Pale,' the 'Pink Panther' theme and, more recently, 'Lady In Red'. Extra points could be given for two or more different colours in the same song title, for example, 'Three Cheers For The Red, White And Blue', 'Cherry Pink And Apple Blossom White', 'Ebony And Ivory' or 'Red Roses For A Blue Lady'.
● If time permits, let the children listen to some of these songs.
● Another such activity could involve the listing of as many singers or groups with colours in their names as possible; for example, the sixties produced groups such as 'Rainbow', 'Pinkerton's Assorted Colours', 'The Swinging Blue Jeans', 'Deep Purple', 'Pink Floyd'. 'Tangerine Dream', 'King Crimson', 'Moody Blues', and others. More recently, 'Simply Red' and 'Deacon Blue' have become prominent in the modern pop world. No doubt family and friends will remember others.

Activity 8: Rainbows
● If possible, observe a rainbow in the sky and discuss how it is formed. Otherwise, or in addition, make a 'rainbow' in the classroom.

What to do:
Take a shallow dish and place it near a sunny window. Fill it almost to the top with water, and insert a mirror into the dish, leaning it against its side so that the sun shines through the window onto the mirror. Watch the ceiling, or hold up a sheet of white paper so that the sun shining on the mirror is reflected onto the paper.

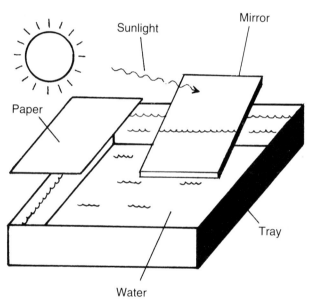

Making a rainbow

● Explain the results of the above investigation: when sunlight passes through droplets of water, it splits up into seven main colours, occurring in a particular order, which we call the colours of the rainbow. Scientists call sunlight 'white light'; all white light can be broken up into its constituent colours in this way. Draw further diagrams to help explain the passage of light through a water droplet:

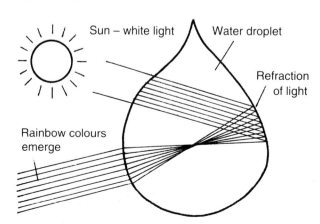

How raindrops split sunlight into a rainbow

● Experiment with glass prisms. White light shining through glass with sharp angles is broken up in the same way.

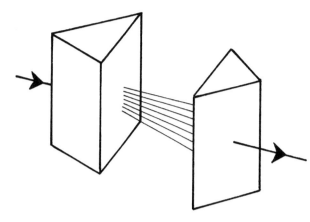

Prism A splits white light into its colours. Prism B converts this back to white light

Activity 9: A colour wheel
● Explain that the rainbow colours form what is known as a spectrum. Reinforce this idea by making a colour wheel, using **Copymaster 3**. Children should be

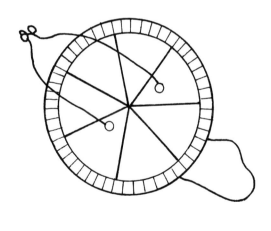

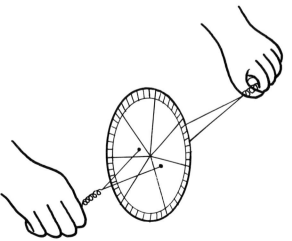

Spinning the colour wheel

101

asked to colour the seven segments of the wheel, one in each of the rainbow colours, in the correct order. Colour the border in rainbow coloured stripes. The wheel can then be cut out and mounted on a piece of stiff card of the same size. Next, the children should make two holes in the circle, about 2 cm apart on either side of the centre, and push the ends of a piece of thin string a metre long through the holes. The ends of the string should then be knotted and the wheel is ready to spin. The circle should be turned round and round so that the string is twisted. Then the hands should be pulled apart so that the wheel spins until the string goes slack.

As the wheel spins, the rainbow colours are blurred before our eyes, making 'white' light – which will probably appear more grey than white!

Note: this activity is not always as successful as it might be, yet is worth trying – at least to show how the colours blur and merge as they pass before our eyes. An alternative way of completing this activity is to make the coloured wheel like a record disc and spin it by 'playing' it on a record player.

• Let the children make other coloured spinning discs, experimenting with using just two or three colours in each case, to see what happens when the chosen colours are merged. Ask the children to predict what might be the result before the discs are spun. They may, for example, predict that a spinning of yellow and red will produce orange – test to see whether the results tally with what happens when paint colours are mixed (see Art, Activity 19).

Activity 10: Experiments with colour
• Set up a series of experiments with coloured filters. Collect together some filters, such as cellophane sweet wrappings, coloured plastics and acetates. Suppliers of theatrical lighting equipment may well be able to supply a variety of coloured filters at a reasonable cost. Fitted

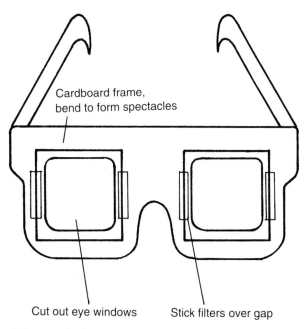

Cut out eye windows   Stick filters over gap

Filter spectacles

into card OHP transparency frames, these filters let the children devise investigations to see how the colours of objects change when viewed through other colours. This could be done simply by holding the coloured filters up to the eye, by making filter spectacles, or by making a more elaborate colour box. Conduct controlled experiments using one or more of these methods to see whether filters of the same colour always have the same results on a range of other colours.

Experiment with putting the same colour over each eye, then two different colours.

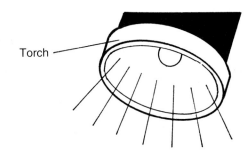

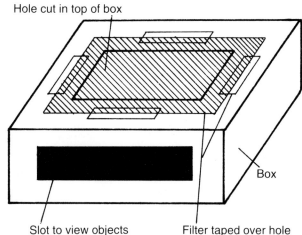

A filter box

Background information
Filters allow only light of the same colour to pass through. They stop light of other colours. Coloured filters change the colours of things seen through them. There is great value in noting changes and seeing whether in fact there *is* a change, without necessarily explaining it at this stage. In the filter box, the filter absorbs some of the colours of the light before it strikes the object. The object then absorbs some more colours and reflects the rest to our eyes. With filter spectacles, white light strikes the object, which absorbs some and reflects the rest. The spectacles absorb some more colours. But the net result is the same.

• Discuss what we mean by 'changing' colours. Ask the key question 'Is what you are looking at literally now a different colour?' The explanation of this in scientific terms may well be beyond the children's comprehension, but it will suffice for them to understand that the actual colour of the original object in white light has not changed. Its colour appears different to our eyes because some of the colours reflected by it are absorbed by the filter.

Background information
We see things because of light. Light 'bounces off' objects to our eyes in a process called reflection. The colours we see depend on the colours that are reflected off objects into our eyes. For example, a red apple looks red because it reflects red light and absorbs the other colours of the spectrum. If an object absorbs all colours, then no light is reflected, and we see black. If an object reflects all colours, then we see white.

● Investigate the effects of mixing coloured lights for stage lighting. Discuss the fact that coloured lights are often mixed together in different ways to create 'atmosphere' and special effects. On stage, colour filters are put in front of white spotlights to light up performers. Either set up a cine projector and place coloured acetate filters in front of its lens to see the results on a backcloth of a specific colour, or experiment with mixing colours and projecting them on slides in a slide projector. Carry out this latter suggestion by taking photographic slide mounts and pieces of coloured cellophane. Stick an appropriately sized piece of cellophane on a mount, place it in the projector and project it onto a white screen. Remove the slide, overlap the cellophane with a piece of another colour and view the results of the mix. Experiment with a variety of colour combinations.

Activity 11: Botanic colours
● Consider the colours of nature, perhaps plants in the first instance. Ask the children's opinion on what they think is the most common colour in the plant world. This could well lead to a study of chlorophyll in plants and a discussion of why almost all plants need 'green' elements in order to live. Use **Copymaster 4** to deepen an understanding of the colours of flowers. This Copymaster provides excellent practice for children in the use of reference material. Ask them to look up, if they do not already know, the usual colours of the flowers shown. Consider what seem to be the most common colours for flowers, and why few flowers are green, brown and black. Ask the children to suggest why many flowers are very brightly coloured, and what advantage this has for them. They could colour the pictures.

Activity 12: Colours for camouflage
● Talk about the importance of colour in the animal world, notably for warning and camouflage. Find out the names and habits of some animals which change their colour at certain times of year for survival purposes, for example, animals of arctic regions which grow a white pelt in winter for protection and camouflage against the snow.
● Discuss why many animals have fur or skin which is rather dull in colour, whilst birds (parrots and peacocks, for example) and butterflies tend to be very brightly coloured.
● Read about and find pictures of the chameleon, an animal noted for changing its colour. Discover how and why the chameleon does this.

Background information
The chameleon changes its colours for camouflage purposes by changing the size of spots of pigment in its skin.

Activity 13: What colour is the sky?
● Observe the sky in a systematic way over a period of time and record colours seen, of clouds and the sky itself. See whether different cloud colours are associated with particular cloud shapes, and with weather patterns which follow. Consider the question: can sky colour help to predict the weather? Is there any truth, for example, in the saying 'Red sky at night, shepherd's delight; red sky in the morning, shepherd's warning'? Put it to the test.
● Observe sunrises and sunsets, if possible, and compare colours seen. Children may well have to do this at home and report findings to the class.
● Investigate why the sunrise and sunset look red, whilst the sky usually appears blue. Fill a glass jar with cold water. Add two teaspoons of milk or coffee whitener. Shine a torch onto the water from above and observe: the water at the top looks blue or grey. Now hold the torch behind the jar and shine it through: the water now looks orange-pink in colour. The effect is more easily seen in the dark.

A sunset in a jar

Background information
The Earth's atmosphere contains microscopic particles of dust and water droplets. When sunlight strikes these particles, the light bounces off them and scatters. The milk in the jar of water has the same effect of scattering the light. Blue and violet light scatter the most, while orange and red scatter the least. At sunrise and sunset, the sun's rays travel through a denser layer of atmosphere than at midday, because the sun is low in the sky. Most of the blue light is scattered in all directions. Red and orange colour is predominant in the light that reaches us directly. At midday, less light is scattered because the sun is high in the sky and more blue light can be seen. The torch in the experiment

replicates this effect. When the torch is held over the water 'high in the sky', the water looks blue. When the torch shines at a lower angle, the water looks orange. If you use a tall jar and shine the torch from above, the water appears blue at the top and pink-orange at the bottom.

● Find out more about how a colour TV screen operates, by researching in books on the subject. The picture is actually made of minute dots of light, in the three primary colours of light – red, blue and green. From a distance, these merge to produce the illusion of a multi-coloured picture.

Activity 14: Computerised colour
● Schools with access to computers with a VGA colour system may be able to obtain and make use of display programs known as fractals – colourful screens of constantly changing kaleidoscopic patterns and effects which fascinate the eye. Computer buffs on the staff may wish to explain as simply as possible the scientific principles involved in such programming. Younger children will doubtless be content to enjoy these effects for their own sake, though it may be possible for older children to attempt some simple colour display programming of their own.
● There are a number of image-processing packages for schools (such as 'Image' for the BBC microcomputer by Cambridge University Press, or 'Imagine' by Topologika for the Archimedes/A3000) which allow colours to be mixed, and textures and patterns to be designed on the computer screen.

Packages are also likely to be available for other computer systems, and these should yield some interesting contributions to the topic of colour.

HISTORY ▶

Activity 15: Newton and the colour wheel
● Research the life and work of Sir Isaac Newton. The splitting of white light into the rainbow colours was first observed and noted for its significance by Newton in 1665 when carrying out experiments. In particular, find out why some scientists refer to the colour wheel as described in Activity 9 as a 'Newtonian disc'.

Background information
Newton recorded his work on white light in the following words:

'In a very dark Chamber at a round hole about one-third part of an Inch broad made in the Shutter of a Window I placed a Glass Prism, whereby the beam of the Sun's Light which came in at that hole might be refracted upwards towards the opposite Wall of the Chamber, and there form a coloured Image of the Sun.'

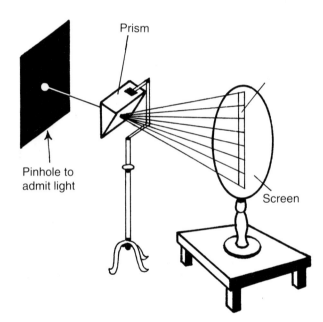

The dividing of white light into the rainbow colours was first observed and noted for its significance by scientist Isaac Newton in 1665 when carrying out experiments

HEALTH EDUCATION/SCIENCE ▶

Activity 16: How do we 'see' colours?
● Explore how we 'see' and why some people cannot see colours as well as others. As well as writing about this, children could be shown how colour blindness tests are done – ask your school nurse if this could be arranged. This activity should of course be treated with sensitivity: if any pupils in the class happen to be colour blind, they should not be made to feel deficient in any way.

Background information
Colours are seen because we have 'cones', cone-shaped cells found in the retina at the back of the eyeball. Each eye possesses around 7 million cones. A certain type of cone responds to red light, another type to green light, and yet another type to blue light. Cones 'see' their light colours and communicate messages to the brain which tell us what we are seeing. People who are colour blind cannot tell the difference between certain colours. In

particular, they may have difficulty in differentiating between reds and greens.

- Let the children devise their own methods of testing for colour blindness. Check the results of these by using 'official' tests borrowed from the school nurse.
- Relate work on colour blindness to investigations into animal eyesight. Very few people are 'colour blind' in the sense that they see only black and grey. Many animals, however, (for example, horses, dogs, cats,

cows) cannot see the range of colours that humans see – they see a world of black, grey and white.

Set up experiments to see whether birds are colour blind. For example, set out foods dyed in different colours (using edible food colourings) on a bird table, and see whether they show preference for any particular colours over a sustained trial period. As an alternative, arrange an investigation to see whether birds prefer to feed from a dish of any particular colour.

ART

Activity 17: CIY – colour it yourself

- Divide children into groups and ask them to imagine they are interior designers for a new house. Provide specifications for the house – perhaps room plans, sizes, positions of windows, aspect, etc. Ask each group to prepare plans for decorating and soft furnishing the house, and to present them in whatever form they choose (written statements, diagrams, colour samples, fabric samples, etc.). Children may be given access to paint charts, wallpaper books, fabric and carpet sample books to assist them, or they could be asked to design their own materials. Finished plans should be displayed so that the whole class can enjoy seeing the ideas and designs of other groups. In briefing the children for this activity, place emphasis on the need to think about colour co-ordination and contrast, in separate rooms and in the house as a whole.
- Extend the above activity by asking children to think about who might like to live in the house they have designed. Ask whether they think their colour schemes would appeal to young and old alike, all through the year, in both winter and summer weather. This links with the idea of colour moods, as discussed in English activities, and the way in which some colours appear to be 'warmer' than others. With older children, explain that more sophisticated research has been done by psychologists on the ways in which colours affect our moods, and that it has been shown that certain room colours have certain effects on the way we feel. For example, blues and greens have a cooling, soothing effect, whilst reds can make us feel anxious.

Activity 18: Colour wheels

- Design and paint decorated colour wheels. The children will need a template based on an enlarged version of the design in **Copymaster 3**. They should draw a pattern/design in each sector, perhaps abstract in nature, then paint or otherwise colour the sectors, one in each of the rainbow colours – allowing for variations in shade of each to make its design stand out.

Activity 19: Colour collections

- Make a collection of objects of one colour – perhaps each group could choose a different colour. Consider the question: how many shades of one colour are there? Try to paint as many shades of a colour as possible. Divide up a sheet of painting paper into twelve (or more)

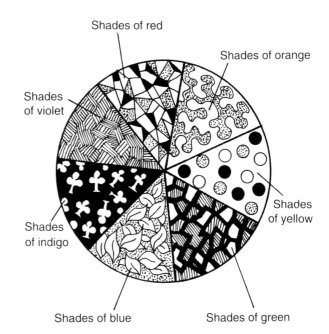

Colour wheel

rectangles. Paint dark blue (or whatever is the chosen colour) in the top left hand rectangle. Continue to paint the sheet by adding small amounts of white to the original paint colour for each successive rectangle, so that they gradually become a lighter shade of blue. End with a rectangle of colour that appears to be white just faintly tinted with blue.

- Investigate the mixing of paint colours in a systematic way. Let children see, for example, how many different colours they can make from the paints available to them. Make recording charts to show what happens when pairs of colours are mixed, then when three colours are mixed. Decide if and when black and white are to be used.
- Discuss whether mixing coloured light gives the same results as mixing coloured paints (link with Science activities). This can be pursued by mixing paints, and by mixing light from torches that have been covered with filters (suggest red, green and blue). Shine the filtered torch lights onto white card in a darkened room and record results so that they can be compared with results of mixing the same colours in paint. Introduce the terms 'primary colours' and 'secondary colours'.

Background information

The primary colours of light are red, blue and green. All the colours of the rainbow can be made by mixing these primary colours. The primary colours of paint are red, yellow and blue. Most colours of paint can be made by mixing these together in various combinations. The colours we actually see are colours reflected by the paints: for example, red paint mixed with yellow paint appears to be orange because orange is the only colour reflected by both paints.

The secondary colours made by mixing the primary colours of light are yellow, dark pink (magenta) and green-blue (cyan). When the three primary colours of light are all mixed, 'white' light is made. The secondary colours made by mixing the primary pigment colours are orange, green and (in theory at least!) violet.

Activity 20: Colour paintings
• Paint animal camouflage pictures, or backgrounds to camouflage scenes upon which a collage creature can be superimposed.
• Paint sunrise and sunset pictures, taking great care to show the range of shades of colours observed in actual scenes, as far as is possible. Superimpose a tree silhouette cut out of black paper for a dramatic effect.
• Consider the power of colour in advertising. Ask the children to go through glossy magazines and study the advertisements, as well as observing large street advertisements – what colours are commonly used?

Extend this activity by investigating which colours stand out best from a distance. Take six poster-sized sheets of paper, all of the same colour. Using large lettering stencils (in the Helix range, for example, available from good stationers) cut an identical short message from papers of six different colours. Stick one message to each of the six poster sheets. Ask six children to stand in the playground holding up the sheets while the rest of the class stand some distance away and try to read the message. Ask the children to move further away from the posters ... and still further ... which colour message can be read from the greatest distance? Repeat this experiment with different colour backgrounds and work out the colour combinations which can best be seen from a distance.

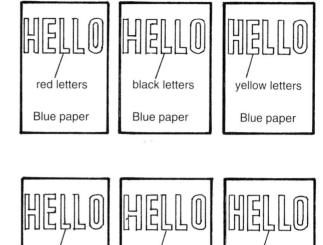

Which colour combination stands out best?

Relate this activity to discussion of colours used for road signs, and the need for these to stand out. (Link to activities in the Signs topic.)

Activity 21: Make your own colours
• Make some colours. Find out more about making and using natural dyes, and dye white material such as old sheets or tablecloths. Use the newly coloured material as a background for embroidery or collage work on the theme of colour. For example, 'colour squares' could be made, where designs are embroidered or appliquéd onto material in the same colour as the background. A line of seven colour squares stitched together, one done in each of the colours of the rainbow, would make a very attractive wall hanging.

Background information
Investigate making natural dyes from the following: onion skins, tea leaves, *Mahonia* berries, lichens, blackberries, red cabbage. Can you discover or suggest any other sources of natural dyes?

Designs should be done in shades of the same colour as the background

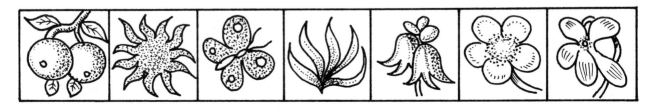

| The red square | The orange square | The yellow square | The green square | The blue square | The indigo square | The violet square |

A rainbow colour line

Activity 22: Tie and dye
● Make beautiful patterns using tie-dyeing techniques. The technique of tie-dyeing is to tie up cloth so that dye cannot reach certain parts of it. The tied cloth is dyed, and when the tie(s) is/are subsequently removed, patterns are left in the dyed material. Cloth treated in this way can be tied with string or stitched as required. During this process, objects such as beans and pebbles can be tied inside the cloth to help create interesting patterns.

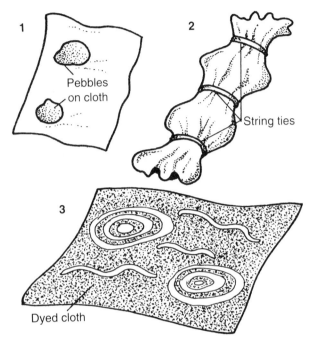

How to make coloured patterns using tie-dying techniques

Activity 23: Chromatography
● Make colour pictures using the technique known as chromatography (literally 'colour drawing'). Cut out flower shapes from blotting paper, and use felt tip pens to colour 'minimal' designs on them. Place damp cotton wool (soaked in water and then squeezed out) on the blotting paper to cover the design, and observe the designs as the colours spread.

Background information
The water spreading from the cotton wool through the blotting paper carries particles of colour from the felt tip pens with it. Often, felt pens have several different colour pigments in them. These spread at differing speeds, so interesting patterns and bands of colour should appear.

Activity 24: The marbling effect
● Take a bowl of water out into the sunshine. Add a few drops of oil to the surface … observe … soon the rainbow colours will be seen, as the sunlight is reflected and split up by the film of oil. Obtain some marbling paint, and create beautifully coloured marbled paper.

Activity 25: Stained glass windows
● Take the children on a visit to a local church to observe the beauty of colour in a stained glass window. As this topic proceeds, they should appreciate how stained glass windows 'work'. As light comes through the window, each piece of coloured glass lets through only light which is the same colour as itself.
● Ask the children to design their own stained glass windows, not necessarily with a religious theme or design. Display them on the exterior windows of the classroom and/or school.

GEOGRAPHY/MATHEMATICS

C5–7

Activity 26: Colour in the community
● Carry out colour surveys in the neighbourhood. Go on a field study walk, with planned investigations. Use **Copymaster 5** as a recording sheet for two sets of data. The top half of the Copymaster is for recording car colours. Children could work individually or in groups, placing ticks or tally marks in each colour box when they see a car of that particular colour (or write further colours in the 'others' box). Conduct counts in a variety of locations and collate data at the end of the activity. Totals can then be transferred to graphs to show pictorially the number of cars of each colour seen by the class (or group). Discuss why a particular colour of car is the most popular – let the children make suggestions about this. (Remind the children of Henry Ford's famous remark, aimed at potential purchasers of his early Model T Ford motor cars: 'You can have any colour you like as long as it's black.')

Discuss the advantages and disadvantages of various colours for cars: for example, many people like red because it can easily be seen, whilst black cars are thought to be more dangerous because they are less easily seen. Ask which colour the children would choose, and why.
● Use the lower portion of **Copymaster 5** to record colours of front doors in a residential area. The sheet gives space for 30 doors to be recorded. Children could work in pairs and the class as a whole could cover a large number of houses. Go along the street, recording the house number in the top left hand square of each box and the colour of the front door in the main part of the box. Collate results at the conclusion of the activity, and draw graphs so that the most popular colours can easily be identified. As with the car survey, this activity can generate a lot of discussion as to why certain colours are popular – perhaps they are bright and welcoming, or do

107

not show up dust and dirt. Let each child talk about the colour of the paintwork on his or her own house, and ask parents why this colour was chosen.

Note: as with all field investigations, the above activities should be undertaken with extreme care for the safety of the children.

● Ask the children to take a careful look at the colour of their skin – an excellent way of leading into sub-topics on people from distant lands and the differing appearances of various groups of the human race. If the class is of multiracial background, so much the better, although even the skin of Caucasians varies considerably – some people have less melanin pigment, and are thus much fairer skinned than others. Discuss why we use the word 'white' to describe the skin colour of Caucasian people. Consider whether this is a good description.

Copymaster 6 shows a variety of people from many nations of the world, all with their own particular colourings of skin, eyes and hair. Use this sheet in association with reference books about distant lands. Pupils should look up the races shown, and colour the drawings as accurately as possible. This activity could be extended by drawing a large wall map of the world, and painting pictures of people from various nations to display in the appropriate place.

● **Copymaster 7** provides a basis for investigating the fascinating subject of eye colour, and for recording data about the eye colours of the children. Help the children to appreciate that the colour of our eyes is one of the characteristics which helps to make us individuals. Nevertheless, eye colours are limited – most are brown, blue, grey or green/hazel. Explain that eye colour is determined by genetic inheritance, although the precise details of how this takes place will be beyond the children's comprehension at this stage. Let the children inspect a partner's eyes. Record the colour of the eyes of every child, and add up totals of the different colours.

Ask each child to do the following. Colour the four eyes at the top of the Copymaster – one blue, one grey, one brown and one green/hazel – and write the class total of each colour beneath it. Draw a graph at the foot of the Copymaster showing the number of children with each colour, in rank order. Label the colours on the horizontal axis.

● A similar activity could be undertaken for the children's hair colour. Furthermore, investigations could be undertaken to see whether there is any correlation between eye colour and hair colour. Extend your sample to include all children (and staff) in the school.

Activity 27: Mathematical 'rainbows'

● This activity may well be useful as a 'spare time' exercise, though it does have a mathematical purpose – if the children can spot it! Ask the children to write down a horizontal line of eleven numerals, *always beginning with 0*. Initially, ask the children to choose a line of eleven odd or eleven even numbers and to increase the numbers by an equal amount each time, since this will ensure that the mathematical aspect of the activity 'works'. Using coloured felt tip pens, draw a semi-circular line to join the two outer numbers together. This arc will form the 'dome' of the rainbow, and should be drawn as high above the line as possible. Repeat the process for the remaining pairs of numbers, working from the outside inwards until all the numbers have been joined up – apart from the single digit in the middle of the line. The final picture should have the appearance of a rainbow (though with fewer than the seven bands of colour that we normally associate with it). Ask the children to do the same with other sets of eleven odd or even numbers. What do they notice about the relationship of the remaining single digit in the middle of the line to the last number on the right? Ask the children to record their discoveries in diagrammatic form:

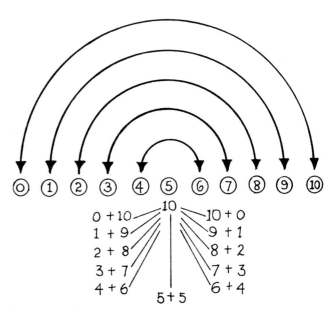

A mathematical rainbow – the story of 10

Background information
The children will discover that when the line ends with an even number, the middle figure in the set must be doubled to equal the last one. Do this with other sets of eleven numerals – does the same principle apply to haphazardly selected sets of numbers?

● Ask the children to experiment with a line of 15 numerals, again remembering to *start with 0*. This will produce a rainbow containing the seven traditional bands of colour – but does it produce a similar effect in terms of the relationship of the single remaining middle number to the one at the right of the rainbow? Once again, ask the children to record their discoveries in diagrammatic form.

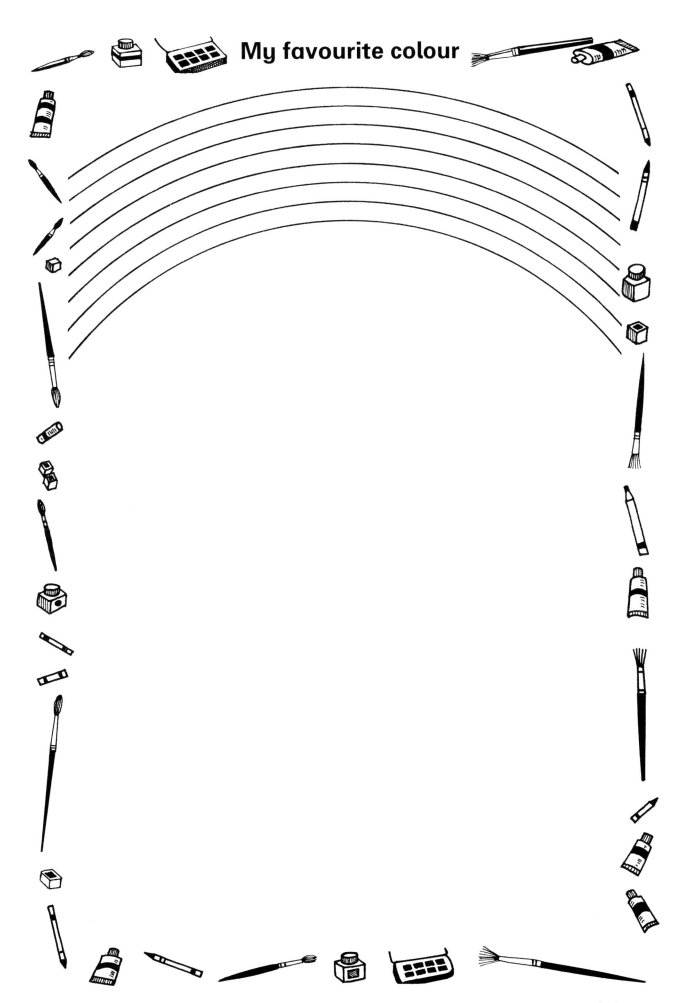

My favourite colour

Colour 1

Colourful moods

happy

hot

summer

sad

winter

lovely

horrible

cold

ill

Colour wheel

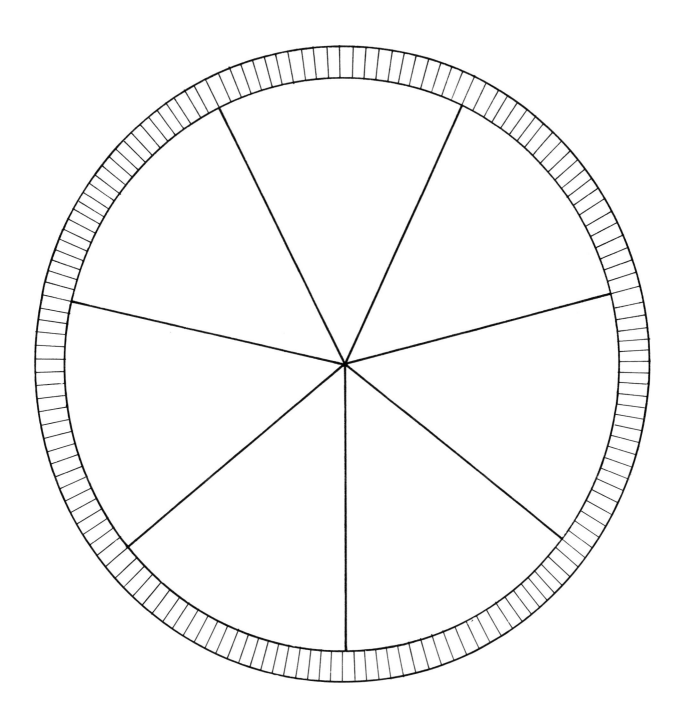

Botanic colours

red   orange   yellow   green   blue   indigo

black   brown   white   violet

daffodil

forget-me-not

delphinium

buttercup

poppy

daisy

rose

freesia

lupin

pansy

violet

dandelion

foxglove

primrose

marigold

bluebell

carnation

 # Colour in the street

	CAR SURVEY	
red	black	yellow
blue	white	orange
green	silver	other

FRONT DOORS

Name of street					

Colour 5

Colours of the world

Japan

Britain

Thailand

Brazil

USA

India

China

Pakistan

Jamaica

Greenland

Africa

Eye colour in my class

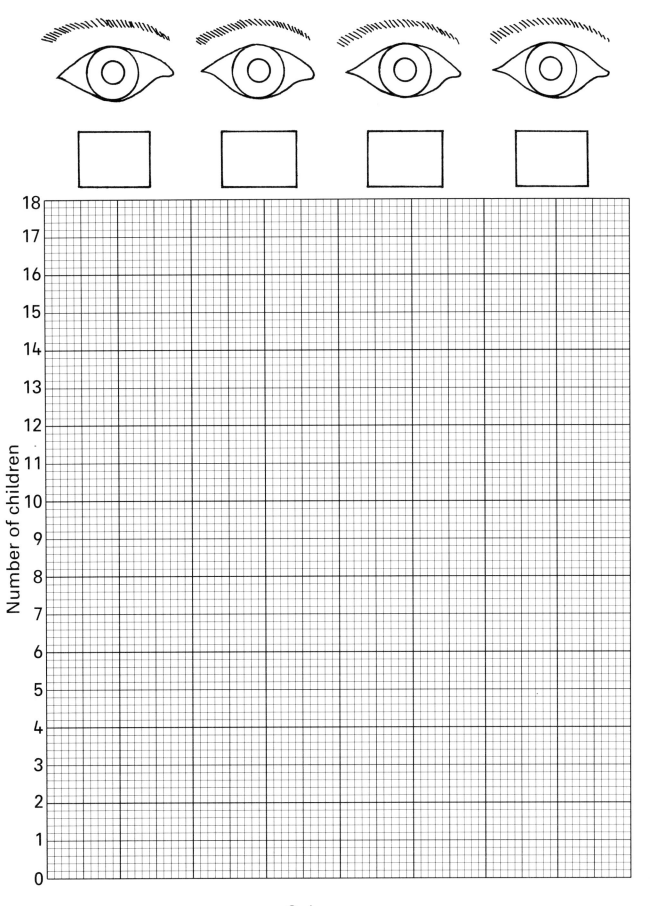

Number of children

Colours

SOUND

Science

- How the ear works
- Vibrations make sound
- Feel sound
- Measuring loudness
- Loud and quiet sounds
- Make sounds louder
- Make an ear trumpet
- Identify sounds
- Sounds of the sky
- Direction of sound
- Make tube telephones
- Animal hearing
- Animal sounds
- Measuring the speed of sound
- Breaking the sound barrier
- Varying speeds of travel
- Body sounds
- How sound is recorded

Music

- Listen to an orchestra
- Identify instruments
- High and low notes
- Play a ruler
- Make a guitar
- Make a xylophone
- Make a drum
- Play a grass reed
- Make musical blow pipes
- Make rhythm shakers
- Instruments from around the world
- Make a balloon orchestra
- Maze of notes
- Synthesizers
- Favourite music and instruments
- Sounds of the decade
- Sound effects in music

Health Education

- Sounds can damage our ears
- Protection from sound

SOUND

History

- Sound in myths and legends
- The wireless telegraph
- Telephones
- The phonograph
- Radio

Geography

- Sounds around the world
- Music of distant lands

English

- Sounds all around us
- Duration of sounds
- Pleasant and unpleasant sounds
- Identifying sounds
- Words to describe sounds
- Sound word stories
- Sounds and our feelings
- Siren warnings
- Sound messages
- Information from sounds
- Life-saving sounds

Environmental Education

- Sound in the world around us – environmental quality
- Noise pollution
- Controlling noise

BASIC CONCEPTS

1 Sounds are all around us. Some we like, some we do not. Some sounds are useful – they give important messages. Other sounds help us to relax and enjoy ourselves, while yet others may annoy us.

2 The ear collects sounds from around us, and helps our brain to 'hear' them.

3 Sounds are caused by vibrating air.

4 Many musical instruments can be made and played to provide a wide range of sounds.

5 The human body can also make many different sounds.

STARTING POINTS

● Listen to everyday sounds all around us, both indoors and outside – quiet sounds and loud sounds, distant sounds and nearby sounds.

● Listen to music of various sorts played or made with a range of instruments, including the human voice.

● Make sounds using everyday materials. Try to find as many ways as possible of making sounds.

● Make a collection of pictures of things that make sounds.

● Make sounds with the body – sing, laugh, shout, cry, click fingers, sigh, hoot, clap, cough, sneeze, whistle, etc.

ENGLISH

Activity 1: Sound is all around us

● Set up a series of investigations into 'sounds all around us'. Allow time for listening, perhaps for a specified period of time, to sounds in the classroom ... outdoors ... in a busy street ... in the countryside .... Note which are near sounds and which are distant sounds, which are loud sounds and which are quiet sounds, which are pleasant sounds and which are nasty sounds. Perhaps duration of sounds could be measured. Record findings systematically so that a wide range of sounds is noted under these various headings. Allow for unidentified sounds! Discuss results. Ask the children's views on sounds they like and sounds they dislike. Is there agreement or disagreement?

● The above activity could lead into some worthwhile linked writing and mathematics. Perhaps graphs could be drawn for each location to show the range and frequency of sounds heard, or the duration of sounds heard could be recorded. Discuss and write about which sounds went on for the duration of the listening period and which were briefer sounds.

● Ask the children to single out which was (in their opinion) the most pleasant sound they heard, and to write some sentences explaining why. Do the same for the least pleasant sound they encountered.

● Make tape recordings (or obtain sound effects records) of everyday sounds, both indoors and outdoors. Play these recordings and see if the children can identify the sounds. Talk about whether this task is more difficult when you cannot see the objects that are making the sounds. This activity could well lead to a discussion on how people who are blind tend to have an extremely well developed sense of hearing, and could probably identify sounds on the tape much more successfully than sighted people.

Activity 2: 'These are a few of my favourite sounds'

● Ask the children to think of and write about 'the best sound I have ever heard' and 'the worst sound I have ever heard', and give reasons for their choices. Share results with the rest of the class: this could help to engender an appreciation of the fact that one person's idea of a pleasant sound could be another person's idea of a nightmare!

● Extend the above activity using **Copymaster 1**, which shows a series of drawings of sounds being made. Ask the children to think about these, colour the pictures, and decide whether they like the sounds or not. They should draw a smiling face by the ones they like, and a frowning face by the ones they dislike. Discuss the results, and again see whether there is a consensus. Point out that there may be many and complex reasons why people like or dislike sounds. For example:

– a noisy aeroplane may be wonderful for Sam, as it signals a holiday
– a noisy aeroplane may be a problem for Jane because she lives near an airport and loses sleep
– the sound of a violin may be heavenly to David, who loves music
– the sound of a violin may be deeply upsetting to Mary, as it reminds her of her dead mother who used to play the instrument.

As well as stimulating discussion such as this, the Copymaster serves the purpose of raising awareness of some of the many objects in our world which make sounds.

Activity 3: Words to describe sounds
• Think of words to describe sounds – perhaps using the above tape recordings as starting points. The results could be compiled into a class dictionary of 'sound words', and may include such words as squeaky, crunchy, rustling, banging, clattering, splashing, groaning, clanking, grating, scraping, clanging and so on. When the dictionary has been compiled, use it from time to time to try and match sounds with suitable describing words. Each word entry could suggest certain objects that make a sound best described by the word in question. Can the words be classified into sweet sounds and harsh or discordant ones?
• Invent new sound words. This activity will cause much thought and perhaps even some frustration, but it could well be that a 'made-up' word seems to capture or describe a sound much better than a traditionally accepted one.
• Write sound word poems or stories, perhaps linking words with the objects that make sounds. Suitable topics could be 'The clanging, crashing bells', 'The roaring, thundering jet', 'The padding, purring cat', 'The wailing, whining siren'.
• Talk and write about how we use sounds to express our feelings. (Link with Science Activity 26 on sounds of the human body.) Write poems or imaginative writing to explain how sounds alone can portray anger, sadness, despair, happiness and fear.
• Write stories called 'Siren Warning', telling of events associated with the wailing of a siren. Perhaps this could be from a police vehicle, ambulance, fire engine, or a wartime air raid warning. If possible, play the children a recording of an air raid warning – one of the most evocative sounds of World War II: perhaps children could bring some family stories about wartime memories connected with this menacing sound. Ask the children to focus in the story on the emotions generated within people by the sound of the siren.
• Write stories about 'The Message', telling of an unexpected piece of news that came as a result of a familiar sound. These stories could be taken from real life, or be fictional in origin: in the latter case, start stories with one of these sentences:

– 'It was a dull, rainy day and no-one expected the telephone to ring ….'

or
– 'The doorbell rang as I was getting ready to go out ….'

Suggest that the children read their stories out loud when they are finished. No doubt some will tell of happy messages, others of sad news, and so on.
• Discuss the role of telephones in modern communication, and how messages can immediately be sent around the world in this way. If possible, find out how deaf people can use a telephone – can you arrange a demonstration of such a specialist piece of equipment, so that the children can write explanations of how it works?
• Following on from the above activity, make a list or diagram to show all the ways the children can think of in which sounds give us information. For example:

Someone wants to talk to us.

Sounds give us the correct time

Sounds tell us about church events

Someone needs urgent attention

I need feeding!

Time to get up!

• Write imaginative stories entitled 'The Sound That Saved A Life'.

HISTORY

Activity 4: Sound stories
• Read or tell the children some of the many myths and legends about sound from around the world – for example, Homer's story of Odysseus and the Sirens from *The Odyssey,* the story in which the geese of Rome saved the city from a barbarian attack by raising the

alarm with their hissing, and the ancient belief that the sound of thunder meant that the gods were angry.
• Introduce the children to some real-life sound stories – the work of Thomas Alva Edison in producing the first phonograph, the forerunner of our modern hi-fi music systems; Samuel Morse and his telegraph code;

the life and work of Guglielmo Marconi, with his 'wire-less' sound transmissions; the gruesome story of Dr Crippen, the first murderer to be brought to justice by wireless telegraphy (1910); and Alexander Graham Bell's pioneering work with the telephone. The more able children may be interested in finding out how these inventions worked, and why the phrases 'tele' or 'phono' are connected with such names.

Background information
Dr Hawley Crippen, an American citizen, came to live in Hilldrop Crescent, North London, in 1900. Unhappily married to a somewhat overbearing wife (an actress named Belle Elmore), Crippen began a relationship with a typist, Ethel Le Neve, who worked in his medical practice. Belle mysteriously 'disappeared' in January of 1910, and in July Crippen and Le Neve took passage on the SS *Montrose* bound for Quebec from Antwerp, disguised as a Mr John Robinson and his son. The ship's captain, H.G. Kendall, noticed that, though he had no luggage, Mr Robinson carried a revolver and claimed to be taking his son to California for the good of his health.

By this time, the police were searching for Dr Crippen on suspicion that he had murdered his wife. Captain Kendall was also suspicious and, believing that Mr Robinson was not who or what he claimed to be, sent wireless signals to another ship, the *Montreal Star*, and to the Reuters news agency. When the *Montrose* arrived in the Gulf of St Lawrence, Crippen and Le Neve were arrested by Inspector Dew of Scotland Yard, disguised as a pilot who had boarded the ship in order to guide it safely into port.

When Dr Crippen's house was searched, the remains of his wife were quickly discovered – she had been poisoned. Crippen was tried for murder, convicted and hanged. The life of Ethel Le Neve was spared, and she lived on alone for many years.

● Dr Crippen's arrest would make an excellent subject for the production of a historical newspaper, with pictures and articles about the crime and its subsequent detection. Highlight the significant part played by wireless telegraphy.

MUSIC

Activity 5: And the band played on ...
● Listen to a tape recording or record of an orchestra playing. In the first instance, listen to this purely for enjoyment – and remember to choose a piece of music that the children will enjoy, perhaps the conclusion of the William Tell Overture, Grieg's 'In The Hall Of The Mountain King' or Strauss's 'Radetzky March'. Identify the music being played, and discuss what the composer and orchestra is achieving through making this sound. Is the music, for example, telling a story, creating a mood, imitating nature? Repeat this experience as often as possible, listening to a wide range of orchestral sounds.
● Ask the children if they can identify any of the individual instruments they can hear playing in the orchestral recordings. Success in this may well depend on the past experience of the children in listening to the sounds of and identifying instruments. As the whole orchestra plays, they may well be able to identify percussion instruments (e.g. drums, cymbals) or to distinguish between sounds made by the different sections of the orchestra – strings, woodwind, brass and percussion.
● Develop the above activity by using **Copymaster 2**, which shows a typical orchestra with its various sections of instruments playing. Talk about the Copymaster with the class, pointing out the various groups of instruments. The activity should be extended by selecting appropriate records or sections of records for the children to listen to, so that they can focus attention on sounds made by individual instruments or

sections of instruments. Pieces such as Britten's 'Young Person's Guide To The Orchestra' can play a useful part in this activity, and there are many other suitably evocative works such as Benny Goodman's 'Bach Goes To Town' or Acker Bilk's 'Stranger On The Shore' (clarinet), Rodrigo's Guitar Concerto, James Galway's recording of 'Annie's Song' (flute), Gerry Rafferty's 'Baker Street' (saxophone), and many more.
● An orchestra can often imitate sounds other than those we associate with music. Play extracts from orchestral recordings such as Rimsky-Korsakov's 'Flight Of The Bumblebee', Haydn's 'Toy' symphony, Vaughan William's *Sinfonia Antarctica,* Mendelssohn's 'Hebrides' overture, and in particular two superb impressions of a railway locomotive, Arthur Honegger's 'Pacific 231' and Brazilian composer Villa Lobo's 'Little Train Of The Kypera', the last movement of his *Bachianas Brasileiras* No. 2. The latter two suggestions may be difficult to find, but are worth the search – try your local record library, or order records/tapes from a reputable dealer. If all else fails, perhaps a blank C90 cassette together with a prepaid envelope and a suitable begging letter on headed school notepaper to the BBC Gramophone Library might elicit a gratifying response!
● Help the children to appreciate contributions made by specific instruments to the overall 'sound' being made by the orchestra. Listening to and playing a range of school instruments will inevitably be very helpful for this activity. Perhaps the children could be blindfolded and asked to identify which instrument is being played.

Activity 6: Musical visits
• If possible, arrange for a specialist musician or a musical group to visit the school to talk about their work and play pieces for the children to hear. Such a visit, for example from a group of ethnic community musicians, would enhance the topic considerably, especially if some of the music could be recorded in a class 'archive'.
• Perhaps a class visit could be arranged to a suitable orchestral concert. Some orchestras do occasionally perform a programme of music suitable for children, and the experience of listening to 'live' music would be a most worthwhile one.

Activity 7: Play a ruler
• Help the children to appreciate that musical sounds are made up of a series of notes. It is of course possible that children of this age may be able to read music to some extent, and so will already have a baseline knowledge of this. Investigate how different instruments produce high notes and low notes, and how they and their players can change the sounds that they make. A good way of doing this is to make some simple musical instruments, thus discovering how stringed instruments, woodwind, brass and percussion all make their distinctive range of sounds.
• Place a wooden or plastic ruler on a classroom desk or table, so that it protrudes over the edge. Hold down the part on the desk firmly, pull down on the protruding end of the ruler and let go suddenly. Listen to the 'twang'. Alter the length of ruler protruding from the desk, making it first longer and then shorter. 'Play' it in each case, and listen to see if the twang changes. Does it make a higher or a lower sound as the length of ruler increases?

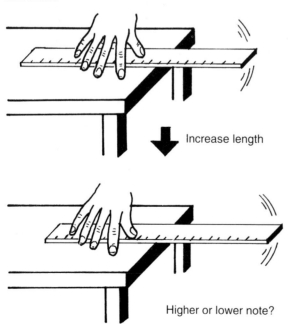

Playing a ruler

Activity 8: Make a guitar
• Make a guitar with a ruler! Stretch a rubber band lengthways over a ruler. Place two short sticks of wood under the rubber band, one at each end of the ruler.

Pluck your guitar. Move one of the pieces of wood closer to the other. Pluck the rubber band again. Does it make a higher or lower sound when the wooden sticks are closer together?

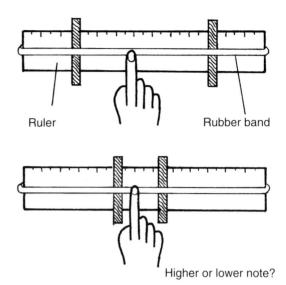

Ruler Rubber band

Higher or lower note?

A very simple stringed instrument

Background information
When the protruding bit of ruler and the 'playing' part of the rubber band are long, lower notes are made. The shorter they are, the higher the notes. This is because they are vibratiing more quickly and the pitch of a sound depends on how fast the thing producing it vibrates. When playing a guitar, the player presses strings to shorten them, thus producing higher notes.

Activity 9: Make a xylophone
• Make a xylophone with a block of wood and some nails. With careful supervision, the children should hammer nails of the same type and size into a block of wood so that they protrude at different heights. Tap each nail in turn with a metal rod or spoon. Find out which nail makes the highest note and which the lowest.

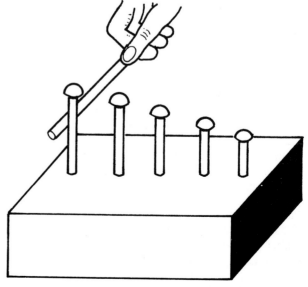

A homemade xylophone

120

Background information

In an orchestral xylophone, lengths of wood produce different notes when tapped. The longer the piece of wood, the deeper is the note produced.

● Make a glass xylophone. You will need six glass beakers, all of the same size and shape. Part fill five of them with water, one almost to the brim and the next four with ever-decreasing amounts. Leave the sixth beaker empty. Play your instrument by gently tapping the sides of the beakers with a spoon. See which makes the highest sound and which the lowest. Play a tune!

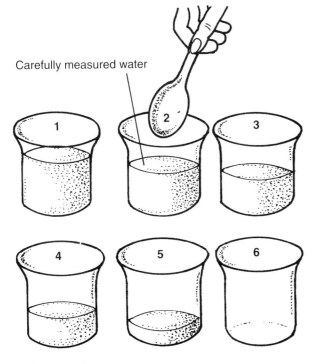

Carefully measured water

A glass xylophone

Background information

The beakers, as drawn in order 1–6, should produce ever higher notes. The amount of water affects the pitch of the sound produced–the more water, the lower the note. Sound is produced because tapping the glass makes the water vibrate.

Activity 10: Make a drum

● Make a drum. Any hollow container such as a box or plastic bowl can be used for this. It will need a drumskin stretched and taped over it, which could be made out of a plastic bag, clingwrap, a balloon or cloth. Experiment by stretching the skin even tighter across the drum to see whether this affects the sound that the instrument makes. A variety of items could be used for drumsticks, such as wooden sticks, knitting needles and rods with corks fastened to their ends.

Background information

The tighter the skin is stretched over the container, the higher will be the note produced when the drum is beaten. This is because the tighter the skin, the faster it vibrates. On orchestral drums, screws or pedals tighten the skin so that the drum's note changes.

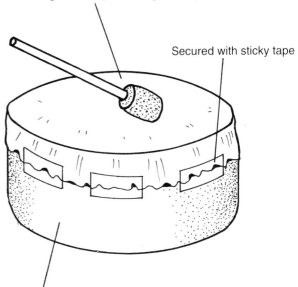

Cling film or a plastic bag over top of bowl

Secured with sticky tape

A plastic bulb bowl would make a useful base for a drum

A drum is easy to make

● Demonstrate the vibration of a drumskin. Place a handful of lentils or rice grains on the top of the drum and gently bang it. Watch the lentils or rice grains leap into the air. Let the children devise experiments to investigate whether a tighter (or looser) drumskin affects the height of the jumping.

Activity 11: Try some other 'instruments'

● 'Play' a thick blade of grass as a basis for understanding woodwind instruments. Hold the grass blade tightly between the thumbs and blow very hard on to it. Hopefully, a noise will be heard as the breath makes the grass vibrate. This is similar to what happens when a player blows on a reed in a musical instrument.

BLOW!

Playing a blade of grass

● Some instruments that rely on the player breathing into them do not have reeds which vibrate. Members of the brass family of instruments depend on the players 'blowing raspberries' or making their lips vibrate like reeds. Make a trumpet: take a piece of pipe, such as hosepipe (make sure it is clean!). Let the children purse their lips and make a 'raspberry' sound into the pipe. See what happens when the lips are pursed even more tightly together. Does the sound coming from the pipe change?

● Make some musical blow-pipes. Take six clean milk bottles of the same shape and size. Line them up and fill them with ever-decreasing amounts of water – starting with bottle 1 which should be almost full, down to bottle 6 which should be empty. Let the children blow gently across the top of each bottle. Does the sound produced by each vary? How does this relate to the amount of water in each bottle?

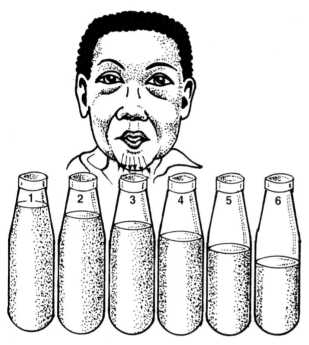

Musical bottles

See how many notes can be made by varying the amounts of water in the bottles. Can the children play a tune? It may help to number the bottles so that if someone is trying to play a tune, a record can be made of the order in which the bottles are blown.

Background information
This instrument makes sounds because air blowing across the mouths of the bottles causes air inside the bottles to vibrate. Bottles with more water and thus less air produce higher notes. This is because a short column of air vibrates more rapidly than a longer one. (Compare this with the 'glass xylophone', where it is the water that vibrates.)

● Make a wide variety of rhythm instruments such as shakers and rattlers by placing objects such as marbles, buttons, pebbles, rice and drawing pins securely into containers such as used washing-up liquid dispensers, yoghurt pots and soft drinks bottles. Different sounds can of course be made by using a range of containers and contents, but a key teaching point of this activity is that each instrument can only produce a single 'sound', i.e. a note of one pitch which cannot be raised or lowered.

Activity 12: Instruments from around the world
● Collect or draw pictures for a book or an A–Z of musical instruments from around the world – how many can you find? See if you can find pictures of an alpenhorn, a balalaika or a zither to start your collection.

Activity 13: A 'balloon orchestra'
● Make a 'balloon orchestra'. Let each child blow up a balloon and hold the air inside by securing the top between thumb and forefinger. Let them then practise using this as an instrument by holding the balloon's neck between thumbs and forefingers of both hands, pulling out the neck into a narrow slit and gradually letting the air out. Practise until a variety of sounds can be made in a controlled way. Organise your orchestra to play low sounds, gradually rising to higher ones.

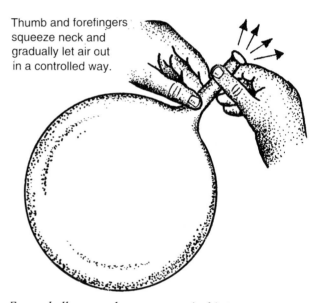

Thumb and forefingers squeeze neck and gradually let air out in a controlled way.

Even a balloon can become a musical intrument

Background information
A balloon 'plays' because the rubber neck vibrates as the air is gradually let out. The resultant sound can be adjusted by tightening or loosening the slit that is letting the air out.

Activity 14: Musical maze
Use **Copymaster 3** as a fun activity when the pupils have spare time to fill during the progress of the topic. Let them follow the musical maze and work out the route from start to finish. As well as the fun factor, this Copymaster provides much useful practice in recognising the shapes of musical notes, which could then be discussed and identified.

Activity 15: 'Artificial' music
● Find out about and illustrate the work of those who work with synthesizers. Can these artists really be called musicians, or should they rather be described as technicians or engineers? Play extracts from the work of artists like the Japanese Isao Tomita. Is this 'real' music?

Activity 16: Favourite pieces

● Ask the children to talk and write about their favourite music, giving reasons for their choice. Ask them to try to describe in words the type of 'sounds' made by this music, and to say what is appealing about them.

● A picture is said to be worth a thousand words, but many people also believe that music can evoke memories and/or pictures in the mind. Perhaps the children can ask their parents, relatives and friends about pieces of music which have special significance. Compile an illustrated class scrapbook of musical memories and, if possible, let the children hear the songs or pieces of music.

● If other teaching colleagues are prepared to become involved in the topic, explain the concept behind the long-running radio series 'Desert Island Discs' to the class, and ask these members of staff to select their eight gramophone records, and talk to the children about them, revealing the reasons for their selection. Play these favourite pieces, of course. (See also Activity 15 in the Leisure topic.)

● At the time of writing, BBC Radio 2 is broadcasting a very successful programme entitled 'Sounds Of The Sixties', in which popular hits of the time are played, some at the request of listeners who write in with stories and other memories of that decade. Let the children hear a selection of 'evergreen' sixties songs, and if time allows, employ this technique with songs of the seventies and eighties. Perhaps an all-time Top Ten for each decade could be selected, based on the votes of the children's parents and friends. This would give scope for some mathematical activity: collating and graphing the results of such a survey, be it within the classroom or extended to include the rest of the school.

When the children have heard some of these songs, ask them to vote on which items they liked best. Once again, results can be collated and graphed.

Ask the children to speculate on which of the recent or current records will become 'Hits Of The Nineties'. How many of today's records will still be played in ten, twenty or thirty years' time? Can the children analyse the mysterious ingredients which go to make an all-time chart success? And are they aware of any artists who began, for example, in the sixties or seventies and are still well known at the present time? If so, why have these performers remained successful for so long?

● The children could paint or construct a montage or collage picture of some of the famous groups of today and yesteryear. Consult appropriate reference books and try to find out which is/are the highest selling record/s ever released, or which vocalist/s have sold the greatest number of records during their career/s. Collate and graph the results.

● Ask the children to say which, in their opinion, is the most beautiful sounding musical instrument, and to give reasons for their choice. Once again, collate and graph the results. This activity could also be extended throughout the rest of the school, giving the children practice in framing the words of suitable survey questionnaires, as well as recording the results.

SCIENCE

Activity 17: How do we hear sounds?

● Use **Copymaster 4** as a basis for discussion and learning about how human beings hear sound. The Copymaster shows the outline of a human ear, and pupils may well be surprised to find out how complex and delicate this organ is. The part that they are used to seeing certainly does not reveal the ear's complexities. Talk with the class about parts labelled on the Copymaster: in the first instance, the three sections of an ear – the outer ear, the middle ear and the inner ear. Let pupils use magnifying lenses to take a look at the ears of their friends, establishing that only the outer ear can be seen. The rest is inside the head. Remind children not to poke anything inside their friends' ears when they are looking! After discussion and research in other specialist books on hearing or the human anatomy, ask the children to colour the Copymaster and write sentences explaining the function of the ear parts that have been labelled.

Background information
The outer ear is funnel shaped. It serves to 'collect' and direct sounds into the ear. Sounds come to the ear as vibrating air. This reaches the eardrum, a thin sheet of skin, which itself vibrates.

In the middle ear are three small bones, known as the hammer, the anvil and the stirrup. These amplify the vibrations from the eardrum.

In the inner ear, the amplified vibrations from the middle ear are changed by the cochlea into electrical messages. These messages are then transferred along nerves to the brain, where they are interpreted so that we actually 'hear' the sounds.

● Explain further the role of vibrations in sound. This can be demonstrated by banging a drumskin and watching rice grains leap into the air, as described in Music, Activity 10.

Background information
Things which produce sound all make vibrations, i.e. they make air shake very fast. If we detect these vibrations, then we hear sound. Vibrations passing from one molecule of air to another are called sound waves. In order to establish the word in the class vocabulary, let the children hear the Beach Boys' record of 'Good Vibrations', one of the seminal 'Songs of the Sixties'.

● Help the children to be able to 'feel' sound. If they hold their fingers gently against their throat while they speak or sing, they should feel the vibrations of their vocal cords. Explain that moving air makes the vocal cords vibrate, which produces the sound of a voice. The shorter the vocal cords, the higher will be the pitch of the voice. (Link with Music activities.) Feel the sounds made by a hi-fi system by holding an inflated balloon lightly in front of one of the loudspeakers. Let the children devise experiments to ascertain whether different sounds (i.e. from different kinds and volumes of music) produce noticeably different vibrations.

Activity 18: How do we measure how loud a sound is?
● Find out about how the volume or loudness of sound is measured, using **Copymaster 5** for discussion and recording of information. Explain that the loudness of a sound is measured in units known as decibels. The Copymaster provides pictures and information about examples of sounds on the decibel scale. Ask the children to think about the sounds depicted, and make intelligent guesses about how they would be ranked from quietest to loudest. Rankings should be written in the space below the drawings. The actual decibel count ratings of the eight sounds are given at the foot of the page. Children can again make intelligent guesses to match the decibel count with the sound and write the answers in the boxes alongside the ratings. Check guesswork with correct answers, which are:

1 Rustling leaves, 10 decibels
2 Whispering, 20 decibels
3 People talking, 50 decibels
4 Vacuum cleaner, 70 decibels
5 Traffic, 90 decibels
6 Pneumatic drill, 100 decibels
7 Disco, 110 decibels
8 Jet aircraft, 150 decibels.

● Ask the children to think of and write about the loudest sound they have ever heard.
● Make lists of 'loud' sounds and 'quiet' sounds. See how many really quiet sounds the class can think of.
● Make sounds louder by constructing an ear trumpet. Roll a large sheet of thin card into the shape of a cone. Cut off the small end of the cone to make a small hole, and hold this end to your ear. The cone should then act to 'collect' sounds and make them sound louder. Turn the ear trumpet into a megaphone: speak loudly into the small hole and your voice should sound much louder to your audience.

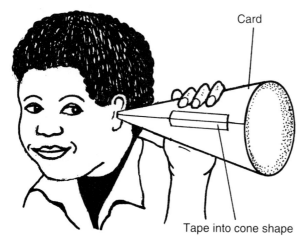

Card

Tape into cone shape

An ear trumpet makes sounds louder

Activity 19
● Test the pupils' ability to identify sounds. Let them work in pairs, one to be tested and the other to collect a range of materials that can be used to produce a sound (e.g. tissue paper, glass, metal, water, clingwrap, balloon, etc.). Children should sit with a cardboard screen between them while one of them makes a range of sounds with the materials and the other tries to guess them.
● If possible, obtain and play recordings of sounds so that the above activity can be extended. Consult your local library for advice on the availability of records or cassettes of sound effects. BBC Enterprises have a series of such sound effects records which may still be commercially available. These could then be used to set up a class quiz, to see who can identify the largest number of sounds. (Link with English, Activity 1, on recording your own sounds.)

Activity 20: Sounds of the sky
● Focus on 'sounds of the sky' to encourage children to use their imaginations and think of as many things as possible which make sounds above our heads. Such sounds could of course be identified from general sound effect collections as suggested previously. Use **Copymaster 6** as a recording sheet for this activity. Children should identify the items shown which make a sound in the air (bee, bat, Concorde, thunderstorm, owl) before colouring them, researching the kind of sound made by each, and accompanying the sheet with explanatory writing on how that sound is made. Spaces between the drawings on the Copymaster can be used for drawing other things that make sounds in the air. Encourage the children to think creatively, rather than merely drawing, for example, various kinds of birds.

Activity 21: Sound games
● Set up tests or games to see whether the children are good at identifying the direction from which a particular sound is coming. The person being tested should be blindfolded, and others can make sounds around him or her, to see if the direction of the sound can be identified. Ask the person to point in the direction from which they think the sound has originated. Investigate whether accuracy can be maintained using only one ear (place a pad of cotton wool over the person's other ear). Record results, and draw graphs to show which child scored the highest number of accurate direction pointings.

Activity 22: Tube telephones
● Make tube telephones. Take a length of plastic tubing – clean garden hosepipe will serve – and insert a plastic funnel into each end of the pipe. Two children will enjoy communicating with each other while in different parts of the classroom, taking it in turns to speak quietly into one funnel while the other person listens at the other end. A similar item of equipment can be constructed using two tin cans and a long piece of string. (The string must be kept stretched taut for this one to work.)

A tube telephone

The children may need to devise some sort of code word (such as 'over') to indicate when it is time for the other person to speak.

● Adapt the above device for use as a stethoscope. Place one funnel against the middle of a child's chest whilst a partner listens to the other end.

Activity 23: How do animals hear?

● Find out more about sound in the animal world – how animals hear, the variety of sounds they make and why. Suitable topics for research by individuals and small groups include:

– animal hearing – some animals can hear higher or lower sounds than we can

– animal ears – a rabbit, for example, can swivel its ears to enable it to hear sounds all around it

– animal noises – a study of the words we use to describe sounds made by animals, for example, screeching, barking, purring, bleating, croaking, etc.

– why animals make sounds – to frighten off predators, to attract a mate, to define territory, to communicate fear or contentment, etc.

– echoes – bats, for example, pick up echoes from objects around them, which helps them to find their way in the dark, and to locate food.

Activity 24: The speed of sound

● Measure the speed of sound. Two children will need to work together in order to do this. They will need a pair of cymbals, a long tape measure or trundle wheel and a stopwatch. In an open space, they should measure out a distance of 500 m. One person stands at one end of this space with the stopwatch, while the partner stands at the other end with the cymbals. At a sign given by the stopwatch holder (perhaps a raised hand), the watch is started and the cymbals clashed. The watch should be stopped as soon as the sound of the cymbals is heard. Time should be recorded as accurately as possible. Repeat the trial several times, and take the average of the times recorded. Then repeat the experiment at a distance of 1000 m. To calculate the speed of sound based on the results of this series of trials, children will need to divide the distance measured (500 m or 1000 m) by the time taken for the sound to be heard.

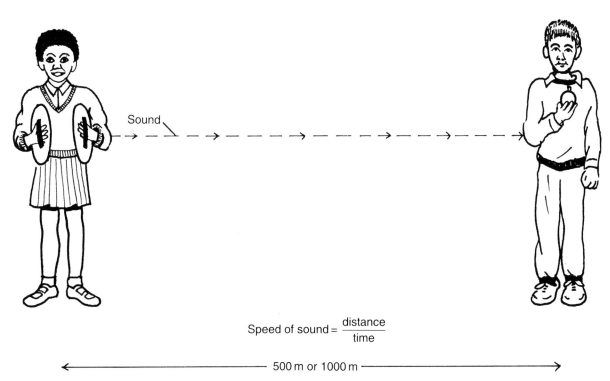

$$\text{Speed of sound} = \frac{\text{distance}}{\text{time}}$$

500 m or 1000 m

Measuring the speed of sound

• Talk about what is meant by the expression 'breaking the sound barrier', and find out more about supersonic aircraft such as Concorde which can fly faster than the speed of sound. (Link with activities in the Flight topic, p.50). Write stories about 'The Sonic Boom', describing imaginative happenings caused by sound shock waves coming from a supersonic aircraft.

• Help the children to appreciate that sound travels more speedily through some materials than others. For example, sound travels five times faster through water than it does through air, and consequently is less attenuated than when passing through air – things sound louder. Co-operate with the children's swimming teacher and, if possible, devise situations in which the children can test this out in the swimming pool by floating with ears submerged whilst listening to sounds made by a partner under water.

Activity 25: Recording sound

• An interesting sub-topic for the children to pursue is the subject of how sound is recorded, and how records, tapes and compact discs are made – particularly if a visit to a local radio station or recording studio could be arranged as part of the topic. Children could even produce a pre-recorded radio programme of their own, with requests, news items, etc., 'broadcast' to the school via loudspeakers or on cassette.

HEALTH EDUCATION

Activity 26: Body sounds

• Ask the children to think of all the sounds that their body is capable of making, without the assistance of musical instruments or other materials. Make a list of these: no doubt the class will be surprised at the extent of such a list. Check it against the suggestions given on **Copymaster 7**. Children should draw their own portrait in the centre of the Copymaster, add any other sounds they can make around the edge in the spaces between those already given, then write a suitable sentence using the word for each sound recorded.

Activity 27: When sound is too loud

• Discuss how very loud sounds can damage the ears, especially when heard over a prolonged period of time.

(Link with Science activities on measuring loudness of sound.) Explain how doctors are worried that young people who listen regularly to excessively loud disco music may be causing long-term damage to their hearing. Make posters explaining this situation to display around your school as a warning to others.

• Find out how people whose work involves continual exposure to loud noise cope with this problem and protect themselves.

• Make some ear muffs and try them out. Try using boxes or pieces of foil shaped into ovals, fixed into a headband with elastic. Elaborate your muffs by lining them with various materials such as cotton wool and tissue paper. Devise a fair test to see which muffs are the most effective.

GEOGRAPHY

Activity 28: Sounds around the world

• Compile a class book or wall frieze entitled 'Sounds Around The World'. Record instances where the 'flavour' or culture of a distant land is captured by indigenous music. There could, for example, be a page or section of the display on musical instruments.

• Make a collection of music from around the world for the children to hear. People often bring back souvenir tapes from foreign holidays, so it may be relatively easy to assemble a collection by seeking contributions from parents and other members of staff. The music of one particular location could then be singled out and used as a starting point for a more detailed study of that distant land, making a worthwhile geographical topic in its own right.

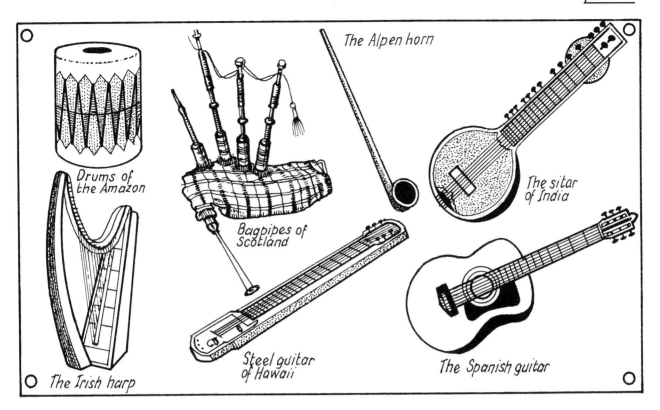

Instruments of the world

ENVIRONMENTAL EDUCATION ▶

Activity 29: Sound and our quality of life

● Introduce discussion about sound in relation to the quality of our environment. Explain how some people's lives are greatly affected by sound, for example, those who live close by an airport, a railway line or station, or a building site. Discuss what could be done to prevent excessive noise. Is it inevitable? Should people have to tolerate loud noise if they find it is affecting their health? What can be done if you are living next door to a really noisy family? Organise a class debate on choosing a site for building a new airport, with panels of children arguing from various different viewpoints – those of the builders, the local residents, the local council and so on.

● Make a display entitled 'Noise Pollution', demonstrating various sources of noise which could be regarded as 'pollution' in our world. Discuss whether we could live our lives without the things that are creating the noise.

● If possible, find out about the work of the Noise Abatement Society, and that of your local Council's Environmental Health Department.

Sounds good or bad?

Do you like it  or not ?

Sound 1

Orchestra

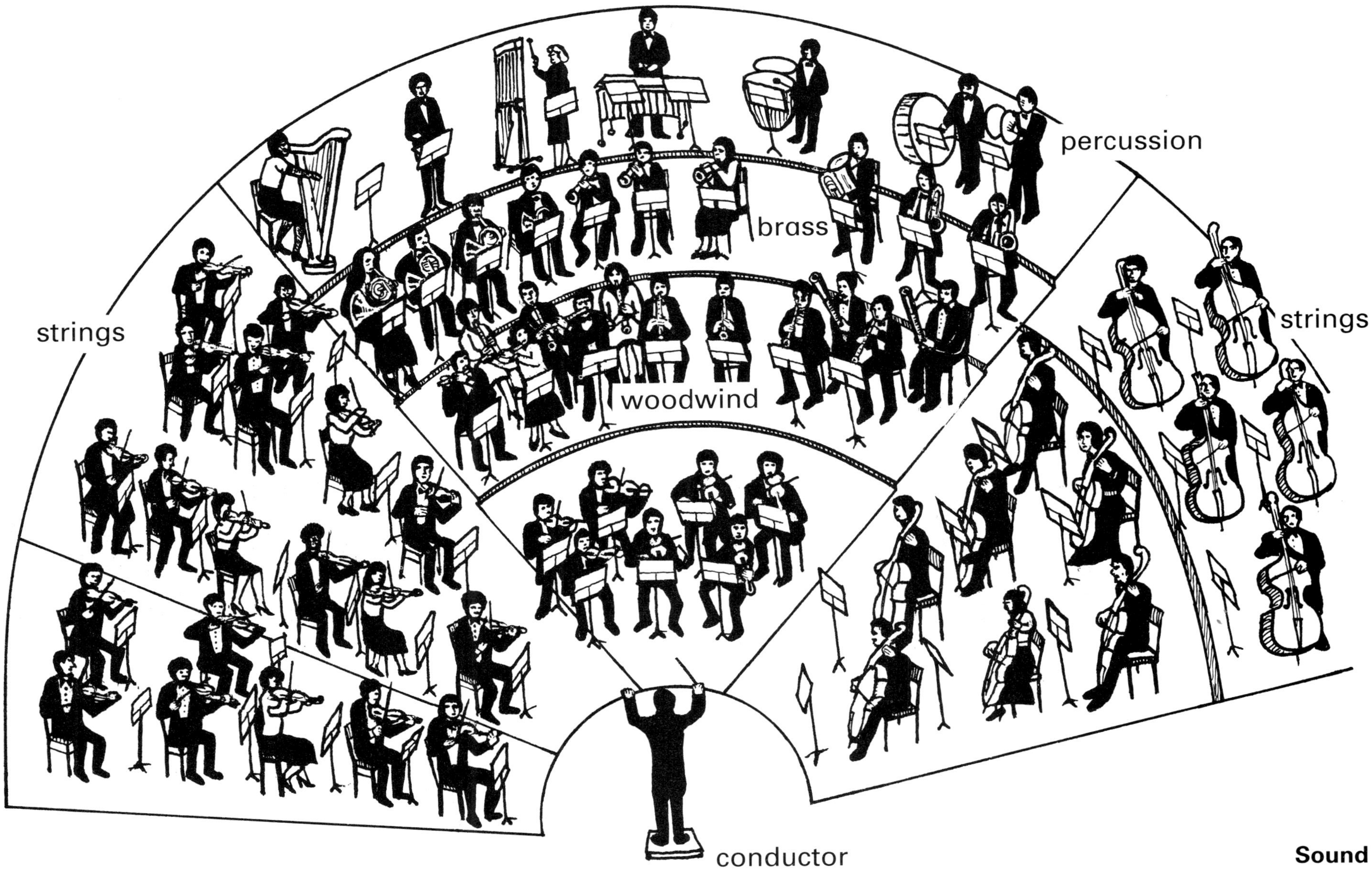

strings

percussion

brass

woodwind

conductor

strings

Sound 2

Amazing notes

Start

Finish

The ear

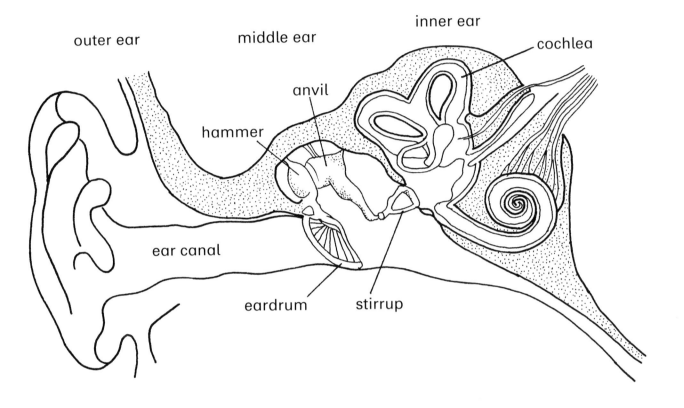

outer ear

middle ear

inner ear

cochlea

anvil

hammer

ear canal

eardrum

stirrup

Measuring sound

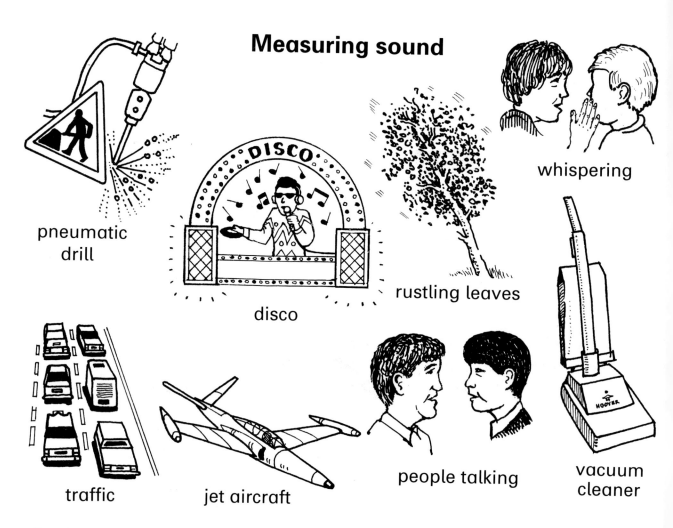

pneumatic drill

disco

rustling leaves

whispering

traffic

jet aircraft

people talking

vacuum cleaner

Rank these sounds in order of loudness. How many decibels?

1 _____ ☐ decibels

2 _____ ☐ decibels

3 _____ ☐ decibels

4 _____ ☐ decibels

5 _____ ☐ decibels

6 _____ ☐ decibels

7 _____ ☐ decibels

8 _____ ☐ decibels

Decibel count 10, 20, 50, 70, 90, 100, 110, 150

Sounds of the sky

Sounds like me

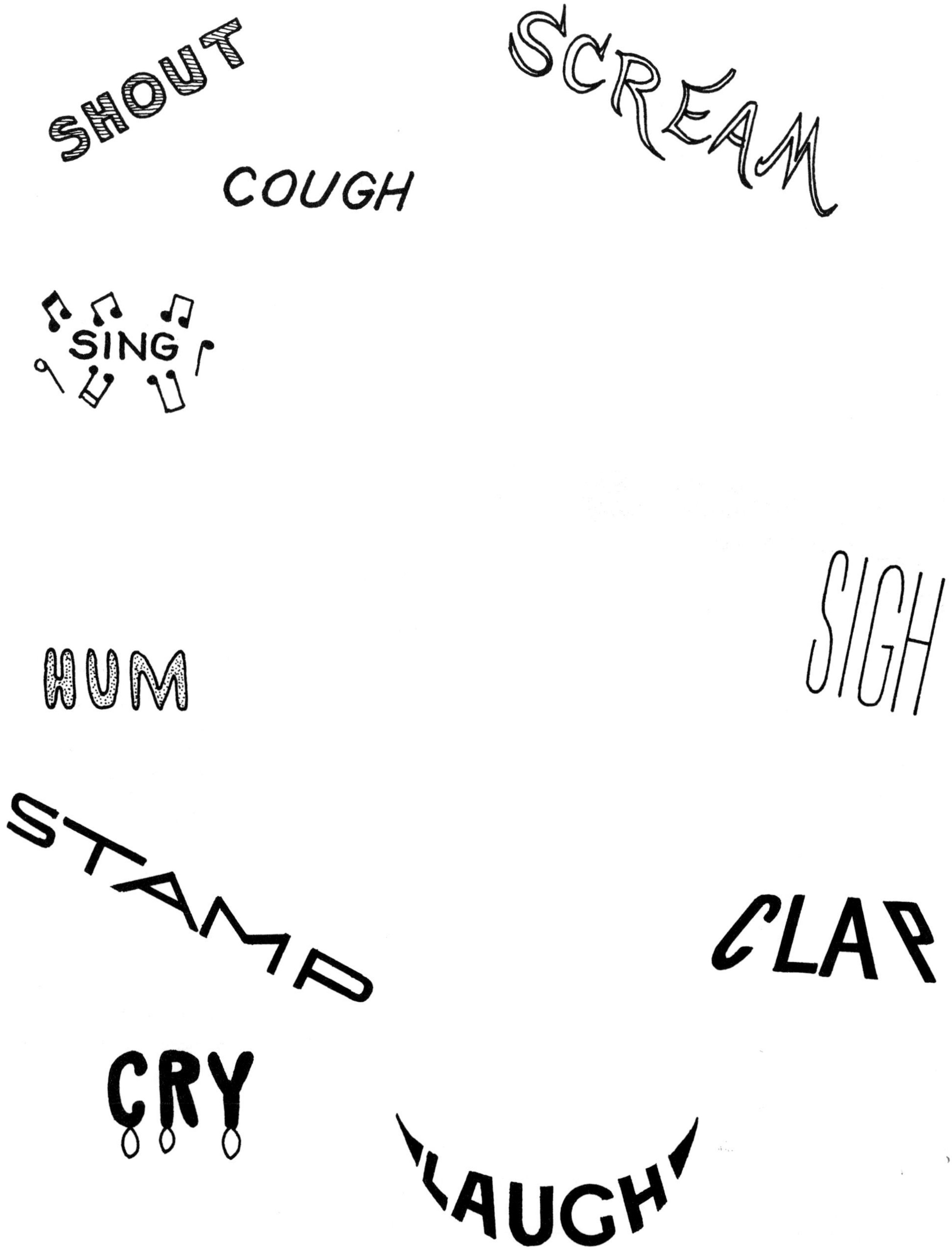

SHOUT

SCREAM

COUGH

SING

SIGH

HUM

STAMP

CLAP

CRY

LAUGH

SPACE

Science/Technology

- Galaxies – the Milky Way
- Naming the planets
- Physical properties of planets
- Planet quiz
- Origin of the universe
- Possible ending of universe
- Galaxy shapes
- Seasons of the year
- Composition of the Sun
- Eclipses of the Sun
- Sun facts
- Moon landings
- Moon facts
- Craters and meteorites
- Phases of the Moon
- Technological links with space
- Rocket technology
- Life in space
- How stars are made
- Death of a star
- Supernovas
- Space station of the future
- Mauna Kea observatory, Hawaii

English

- Astronomical dictionary
- Messages for aliens
- Space menus
- Life on a Moon mission
- Aliens
- 'Let the Alien In?' debate
- UFOs
- Signs of the zodiac
- Constellations
- Myths and legends about the stars
- Black hole stories
- The future of space flight
- Maze of stars

History

- Discovering a spherical earth
- Famous scientists – Newton, Copernicus and Galileo
- History of space exploration
- What else Neil Armstrong might have said ...
- Space mission timeline
- Halley's Comet

Environmental Education

- Space – common territory
- Space waste

Art

- Fortune-telling pictures
- Galaxy pictures
- Life Beyond Earth frieze
- Display of stars and constellations
- Black hole pictures
- A 3-D solar system
- Model rockets and satellites
- Space in the classroom
- Rocket launch pictures
- Pictures/models of aliens and UFOs

Mathematics

- Sky rocket mathematics

BASIC CONCEPTS

1 The universe is made up of millions of groups of stars, called galaxies. The universe is a term used for the whole of space, as we know it.

2 Some stars have planets in orbit around them.

3 Our own planet, Earth, is in a galaxy called the Milky Way. It is part of a group of planets in orbit around the Sun, called the Solar System.

4 People on Earth have developed and used technology to 'conquer' parts of space. We can now travel to land people on the Moon, and to explore the outer planets of the Solar System and beyond.

5 Space is 'common' ground. It does not belong to any particular nation or group of nations on Earth.

STARTING POINTS

• Begin the topic at a time when there is media coverage of an event relating to space, for example, an eclipse, the launch of a spacecraft, or information from a satellite. Collect press cuttings, and ask the children to look for details on the television news. If possible, videotape appropriate news bulletins or relevant documentary programmes for later viewing in the classroom.

• If possible, observe the sky after dark, when stars can clearly be seen. This may require briefing the children and parents, and asking them to do this at home.

• A good place to start a topic on space is clearly with our home galaxy, called the Milky Way. Collect books, posters and any other resources about this for the children to begin their studies.

• Read horoscopes. Many children will have a general interest in this subject, and will know their astrological birth signs. Explain the link between these signs and the stars in the sky.

SCIENCE

C1–4

Activity 1: Our home galaxy

• With the aid of **Copymaster 1**, explain to the children that the universe is made up of millions of collections of stars, called galaxies. Every galaxy in turn has millions of stars. The galaxy in which we live is called the Milky Way, a gigantic swirl of stars. One huge star in the Milky Way is the Sun, and the Earth is one of nine planets which move around the Sun. **Copymaster 1** shows the nine planets of the Sun in their orbits. Suggest that the children label the Sun and the planets, add any other information they wish on the diagram, and use this as a basis for developing writing on our own Solar System.

Background information
The universe is the term used for the whole of space as we know it, with huge swirls of millions of stars called galaxies. The Milky Way has around 250 000 000 000 stars. Some stars have planets, which are spheres of rock or gas, orbiting around them. The arrangement of a star with its planets is called a solar system. The Sun is the enormous star at the centre of our Solar System, a

gigantic ball of burning gas, which has nine planets in orbit around it. The Earth is the third closest planet to the Sun. Between them, the nine planets of the Solar System have fifty or so moons circling around them. The Solar System also contains thousands of minor planets called asteroids and numerous comets. Stars give off light, but planets do not. They appear to shine in the dark sky because they reflect light from the Sun. We need the Sun to light planet Earth.

Activity 2: Interplanetary tables

• Following on from the above activity, help the children to name the planets, in the correct order, and provide data so that they can draw tables of facts and figures about the planets – their rotational period (i.e. how long they take to spin once around their axis) and their orbital period (i.e. how long they take to go once around the Sun).

This information could be put on a colourful wall chart, or could be written alongside the planets and their names on **Copymaster 1**.

ROTATIONAL PERIOD	PLANET	ORBITAL PERIOD
58.7 days	MERCURY	88 days
243 days	VENUS	224.7 days
23.93 hours	EARTH	365.25 days
24.62 hours	MARS	687 days
9.92 hours	JUPITER	11.9 years
10.23 hours	SATURN	29.5 years
17 hours	URANUS	84 years
18 hours	NEPTUNE	165 years
6.4 days	PLUTO	248 years

Planetary facts and figures

Activity 3: Explore the planets

●   The above chart should provide endless scope for discussion, and further research about each of the planets, their size and position. Perhaps children could divide into groups, each to research one of the planets, finding out as much about it as possible – its physical properties, its diameter at its equator, its orbital speed around the Sun, its surface temperature, the number of its rings (if any), and any other interesting features. Note that the Earth is the only planet in our Solar System which supports life. It is just the right distance away – if it was nearer to the Sun it would be too hot to sustain life, and if it was further away, it would be too cold.

Activity 4: A planet quiz

●   Organise a planet quiz. The following questions may give a helpful start. These could be transferred to work cards, so that the children could work in groups – give each group a time limit in which to research the answers, and award a prize to the group with the highest number of correct answers.

Questions

1. Which is the smallest planet?
2. Name the largest planet.
3 Which is the nearest planet to the Sun?

4. Name the planets with rings.
5. What are these rings made of?
6. Name a hot, stormy, cloudy planet.
7. Which planet has the most moons?
8. Name the planet with two moons called Phobos and Deimos.
9. Name the red patch on Jupiter.
10. What holds all the planets in their orbits?
11. Name a planet with oceans and air.
12. Which planet rotates from east to west, the opposite direction to all the others?

Answers

1. Pluto;   2. Jupiter;   3. Mercury;   4. Uranus, Neptune, Jupiter, Saturn;   5. Ice and dust particles;   6. Venus;   7. Saturn (18);   8. Mars;   9. Giant Red Spot;   10. Gravity;   11. Earth;   12. Venus.

Activity 5: How did the universe begin?

●   Consider the scientific explanation for the origin of the universe, and use **Copymaster 2** for the pupils to record their accounts. Significant events are given down the left hand side of the Copymaster, and the number of years since the 'Big Bang' is given in millions on the right. Suggest that the children draw and colour suitable pictures in the spaces by each named event, and then write sentences explaining each on separate paper.

Background information
This chart refers to the origin of the universe according to the 'big bang' theory. Most astronomers believe that the universe began with a bang, or gigantic explosion, in which a source of amazing energy blew apart, scattering hot gases all around. Galaxies and their stars began to form out of the material deriving from this 'big bang', some thousand millions of years later. It is generally agreed that the universe began around 15 000 million years ago.

Activity 6: How might the universe end?

●   Discuss scientific views on how the universe may end its days.

Background information
Astronomers believe that the galaxies, which are speeding outwards, could gradually slow down and fall back towards the centre of the universe. They would then collide and create another explosion that would end the universe as we know it. All of its material would be crushed together. This cycle of events could be repeated if a new 'big bang' occurred.

Activity 7: Galactic shapes

●   Help the children to appreciate that galaxies come in an assortment of shapes, including spirals, ellipticals, barred spirals and irregular galaxies. (See Activity 30, in the Art activities.) Galaxies in the universe tend to cluster together.

Activity 8: How do we get our seasons of the year?

●   Draw diagrams – perhaps a large one on the classroom wall – to explain that the occurrence of seasons is related to the Earth's orbit around the Sun.

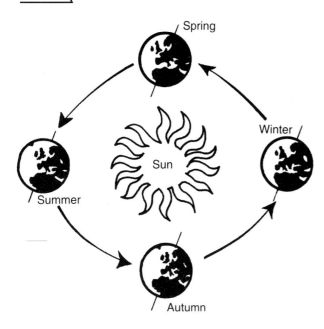

Our seasons are related to the Earth's orbit around the Sun

Background information

The Earth takes one year to move around the Sun, and while doing so it turns on its axis, once each day. The axis of the Earth is tilted to one side. In the Northern Hemisphere, in the summer time, the North Pole points towards the Sun, and northern lands have sunlight for a longer period of time each day. In winter, the North Pole points away from the Sun because the Earth has moved to the other side of the Sun. Lands in the Northern Hemisphere have much shorter hours of sunshine. Because of the angle of tilt and the movement of the Earth, the seasons are reversed in the Southern Hemisphere. While Britain is enjoying summer, it is winter in Australia.

Activity 9: More about the Sun

● Find out more about the Sun, the giant star at the centre of the Solar System. Help the children to understand and to write about why the Sun is crucial in our lives: without it there would be no life on Earth. It provides both light and heat, and its force of gravity keeps the Earth in its position. Draw diagrams showing the layers and components of the Sun. The Sun is mainly composed of the gas hydrogen.

● Add the distance of the Sun from the Earth to the information on **Copymaster 1**. This is 93 million miles, or 150 million kilometres. This distance is known as an astronomical unit.

Background information

The diameter of the Sun is around 100 times greater than that of the Earth. It is estimated that the Sun will survive for a further 5000 million years. As its hydrogen runs out, it will expand and the Earth will be engulfed along with other 'inner' planets. Eventually, the surface of the Sun will be removed into space and the remainder will shrink and cool down. Sometimes, dark patches called sunspots appear on the Sun's surface. These are areas of gas that are cooler than the rest of the surface. The Sun is around 4–6 billion years old, and is in approximately the middle of its anticipated life span.

Activity 10: Eclipses of the Sun

● Investigate why eclipses of the Sun occur – these happen when the Sun, Moon and Earth are all lined up, so that the Moon blocks the light from the Sun.

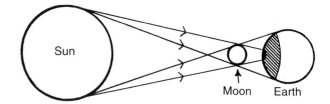

An eclipse of the Sun

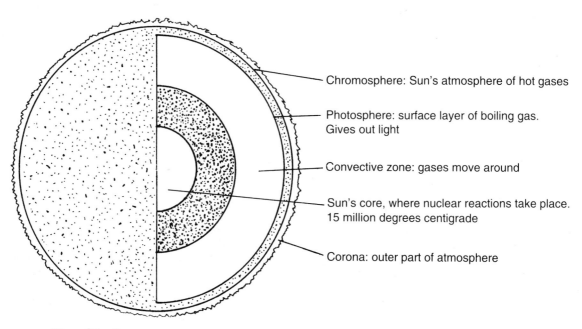

The composition of the Sun

138

Activity 11: About the Moon

● Find out as much as possible about the Moon. This could well be approached by reading and researching attempts that have been made to explore it. Use **Copymaster 3** as a starting point. Children will enjoy colouring this picture, which shows US astronaut Neil Armstrong on the surface of the Moon, together with the craft which conveyed Armstrong and Edwin 'Buzz' Aldrin to the Moon's surface – the Apollo XI spacecraft and the moon lander vehicle, which connected with the main spacecraft. Ask the children to write accounts of the story depicted on this Copymaster, the first Moon walk which took place on 20 July 1969 (US Eastern Daylight Time) or 21 July 1969 (BST). They can add other details to the picture, perhaps the flag of the USA as a reminder of which nation achieved this first triumphant extraterrestrial landing. (Link with History activities on the exploration of space, Activity 35).

Background information
The Moon is 384 400 km from the Earth and is 3476 km in diameter. It has no atmosphere, so the ground gets extremely hot by day (up to 110°C) and far below freezing point at night (down to −160°C). The Moon turns on its axis once in every 27 days, so the land has daylight for around two weeks, then darkness for two weeks. Because of the turning of the Moon, the same side always faces the Earth.

Activity 12: Why are the Moon and our Earth so different?

● Discuss why the Moon and the Earth are so different, when they were both created at the same time and are so close together. Why is the Moon lifeless and frozen whilst the Earth is rich in life? The answer is, of course, because the Moon has no atmosphere.
● Suggest that the children write accounts entitled 'Moon: Silent, Dry Planet', describing the nature of the Moon's silent, arid environment. Because the Moon has no atmosphere, there is no sound. Sound waves cannot travel through empty space. Relate this fact to the experiences of Moon astronauts, who could only communicate with each other through radios.
● Draw sketches or make paintings of the Moon's surface, showing the dusty craters. Explain in accompanying writing how these craters have been made.

Background information
Craters are formed by meteorites, chunks of rubble moving around in space. When meteorites pass close to the Moon, the force of gravity pulls them down and they crash onto the Moon's surface, making craters.

On Earth, we may see meteorites as 'shooting stars'. Usually they are burnt up in the Earth's atmosphere. Sometimes meteorites do fall to Earth, causing a considerable impact on the surface. The largest meteorite ever known to fall landed in Namibia, Africa. It weighed about 60 tonnes and measured 2.75 m × 2.4 m. A famous meteorite crater with a depth of 175 m can also be seen in Arizona, USA. It was formed some 22 000 years ago when a huge meteorite fell to Earth.

Activity 13: The phases of the Moon

● Make a large diagram on the classroom wall to explain the phases of the Moon. The Moon is lit by sunlight. Sometimes we see all of the illuminated side of the Moon – this is what we mean by a full moon. Sometimes we see only part of the lit side, and this we call a crescent moon. As the Moon continues on its travels around the Earth, we are able to see varying amounts of its surface.

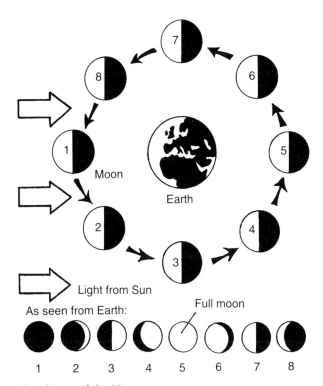

The phases of the Moon

Activity 14: Links with space

● Use **Copymaster 4** as the basis for discussion and further research about the various ways in which we 'look at' and find out more about space, and make connections between the Earth and other locations in space. The Copymaster has been designed without labels, so that the children can investigate for themselves and make suggestions about the objects shown. Suggest that they identify them, label and colour them, then do further pieces of writing about the importance and development of each. The objects shown are as follows.

1 A Satellite The word satellite is used to describe something which orbits a planet, and thus the Moon is a satellite of the Earth. Artificial satellites today have many uses – they relay TV and telephone signals; they study and photograph the Earth, changing weather patterns and the stars. Man-made satellites are boosted into orbit by a rocket, so that they escape the force of gravity.
2 A dish aerial Satellites are able to send information down to Earth in the form of radio signals. These are received on the ground by dish aerials.

139

3 Balloon Balloons filled with hydrogen or helium are sent up into the outer atmosphere to carry equipment for scientific investigations. They are less expensive than satellites, and can be controlled from ground stations.

4 A rocket Rockets can be used to launch other spacecraft and satellites. They are also used to gather information from the upper atmosphere. Sometimes information is sent back to Earth via a parachute.

5 Spacecraft Sophisticated spacecraft such as the USA's *Voyager 2* can travel for years in space, going to the outer planets and beyond the Solar System. Some craft carry electronic messages on board, telling of where they come from and about life on Earth.

6 Space shuttle Unlike rockets, space shuttles are designed to be reusable. The shuttle carries a tank of fuel, used up and then disposed of after take-off. The rest of the craft continues on its mission, then glides back safely to Earth where it can be relaunched.

7 Telescope Telescopes were used to look at objects in space long before the days of rocket technology. Galileo Galilei was the first person to use a telescope for looking at the stars in 1609. Modern telescopes are used to observe stars that are invisible to the naked eye, and are essential items of equipment in observatories.

Activity 15: More about space rockets
● Find out more about space rocket technology, and perhaps chart developments, by consulting specialist books.

Background information
Rockets are able to overcome the gravitational pull of the Earth's atmosphere and launch themselves, their cargo and perhaps travellers into space. Huge amounts of fuel are needed to launch a rocket. Rockets lift off by pushing gas through 'thrusters' which cause them to be propelled upwards at great speed. The Russian scientist Konstantin Tsiolkovsky was the first person to design a modern rocket in 1903. The first test flight took place in the USA in 1928. However, the idea of exploring space might well be said to have become more of a reality following the activities of a group of amateur enthusiasts in Germany who formed themselves into the 'Society for Spaceship Travel' in 1930. One of their members was a 20-year-old student engineer called Wernher von Braun, and he began working on the idea that a new and more powerful fuel than any in existence at that time would be needed to propel rockets into space. He conducted experiments on rocket propulsion in an attempt to create this new fuel, and an early rocket known as *Mirak 1* reached a height of 1200 feet. There was little money spent on this work, however, until von Braun's experiments were financed by the German army and the Luftwaffe during World War II. During the Second World War, rockets were used as weapons, and the German V1s (known by civilians as 'doodlebugs') were targeted on London. Since that time, technology has improved dramatically, enabling rockets to be launched into space.

Activity 16: Life in space
● Write accounts about life in space, and illustrate them appropriately. A good way to start would be by making a life-sized model of an astronaut to stand in the classroom, though children should be helped to realise that space travellers do not spend all their time in suits

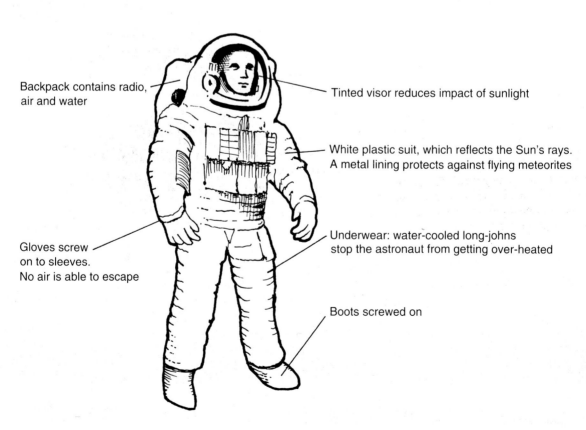

Backpack contains radio, air and water

Tinted visor reduces impact of sunlight

White plastic suit, which reflects the Sun's rays. A metal lining protects against flying meteorites

Gloves screw on to sleeves. No air is able to escape

Underwear: water-cooled long-johns stop the astronaut from getting over-heated

Boots screwed on

The astronaut in his space suit

when in the spacecraft. White plastic material is ideal for the base of the astronaut's suit – easily obtained by using bin liners.

● Consider and write about other aspects of living in space – including coping with weightlessness, planning meals, going to the lavatory, staying healthy and living in confined quarters. (Link with English activities.)

Activity 17: How stars are made
● Find out and write about how stars are made.

Background information
Stars are formed inside huge clouds of gas and dust. Particles of gas gradually drift into each other, and a gigantic ball is formed. Chemical reactions within it lead to a sudden blaze of light, and the star is formed. Children could undertake creative writing entitled 'A Star Is Born', describing the sudden burst of light in the sky.

● Following on from the above, write about the 'Death Of A Star', describing how, as the hydrogen is used up, the star puffs out into a huge glowing mass, many times larger than the original star. The outer surface is eventually blown off and the remainder shrinks and cools. Creative poetry could be written about this sequence of events, perhaps displayed on a star-shaped background which could become part of a 'star' wall display (see Art activities).

● Explain to the children that the scenario described above occurs for the majority of stars. For the biggest and hottest stars in the universe, however, their final demise might be far more dramatic. These incredibly huge and hot stars, called 'blue giants', may be destroyed in a gigantic explosion known as a supernova. Once again, ask the children to write creative poems about such an event.

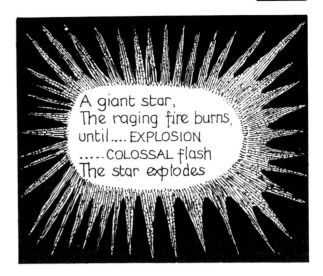

Activity 18: A space station of the future
● Design a future space station, draw a plan or picture, or make a model of it and write about its components for a wall display in the classroom. No doubt your station will be powered by solar panels, which collect light from the Sun's rays and turn this into electric power.

Activity 19: The most powerful eye in the world
● Find out about one or more locations in the world that are famous for their stargazing activities. Make sketches or paintings of well known telescopes or observatories and find out more about their work and how they function.

Background information
Mauna Kea observatory on the Big Island of Hawaii in the Hawaiian Islands is set to become 'the most powerful eye in the world'. The top of Mauna Kea, a non-active volcano, is 4205 metres above the Pacific Ocean

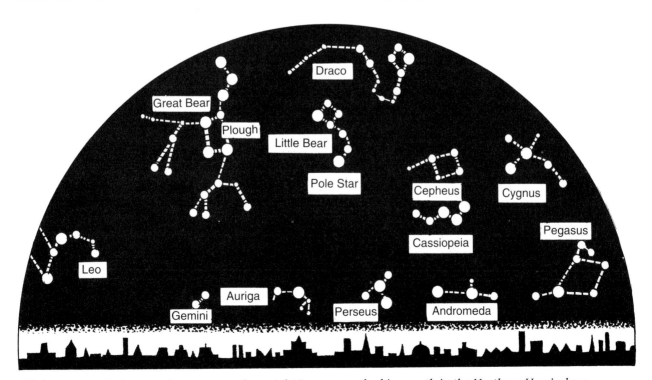

All these constellations can be seen on a clear night in summer, looking north in the Northern Hemisphere

and is the most important astronomical site in the world. A new 10 m telescope will view space with the newly developed technology of 36 hexagonal mirrors. This is the largest telescope in the world. Other large telescopes have traditionally used one giant mirror. The 36 mirrors of the new W.M. Keck Telescope are fitted into a mosaic capable of adjusting itself a hundred times a second. Nine observatories operate on the summit of Mauna Kea, run by the USA, the UK, France, Canada and the Netherlands. They are used by astronomers from around the world. This volcano has unsurpassed viewing conditions. At its great altitude it has clear, dry, stable air. One hundred per cent of the stars of the Northern Hemisphere can be seen from Mauna Kea, and 80% of those in the Southern Hemisphere.

●   Show the children pictures of the constellations they may be able to see on a clear night at various times of the year.

ENVIRONMENTAL EDUCATION

Activity 20: Who owns outer space?

●   Introduce the idea that space is common territory for all nations on Earth. No-one has any particular claim to it or dominion over it. Ask the children therefore to consider and debate whether it is appropriate for a small number of developed nations to 'take over' space in the sense of exploring it and leaving their debris there. Explain that space is becoming the 'junk yard' of the Earth – millions of pieces of rubble from rockets and other space encounters are still orbiting around. The Moon's surface alone currently has the remains of six lunar landing vehicles, several Moon buggies and many tonnes of other debris left by Apollo astronauts. Ask the children's opinions about this, and try to think of ways in which the world can protect this common territory. As a part of this activity, debate the pros and cons of space exploration in general. Is it a good idea to spend such vast sums of money on conquering space? Let the children present and argue their views, and see if a consensus is reached.

ENGLISH

C5–7

Activity 21: Compile an astronomical dictionary

●   At the outset of the topic, begin to make a class book of 'space terms'. Perhaps you could call it an Astronomical Dictionary. Suggest that the children make an entry each time they discover a new space word in their reading and research activities. Each word could have a page of its own in order to accommodate an explanation of its meaning and perhaps an illustration. If the book is made up of looseleaf sheets, it can easily be assembled in alphabetical order.

Activity 22: Send a message into space

●   Ask each child to write appropriate messages that they would wish to put in a spacecraft undertaking an extensive mission beyond the Solar System. The messages should aim to convey details about what life on Earth is like, to any 'aliens' who may receive them. Share the results with the rest of the class. Make up a 'space mission box' containing a selection of the messages, plus any other information the class would like to include – perhaps newspapers, photographs, or music of the Earth. Perhaps they could actually devise and equip a real space capsule with appropriate items for 'launching' into outer space.

Activity 23: A menu for space

●   Design menus to take into space. These can, of course, be creative and imaginative but should take account of the real problems of trying to eat and drink in a weightless place – where drinks cannot flow out of a glass, and where crumbs and small items of food will fly about ….

Activity 24: A Moon mission

●   Write a story about 'Life On The Moon Mission', telling of day-to-day happenings on a spacecraft, the problems encountered in trying to follow a daily routine, as well as the anticipation and excitement of the voyage. Suggest that the story tells of realistic happenings, for example, moving about the craft by pushing off the walls and floating; doing daily exercises on special machines; conducting experiments and observations, and washing in special showers, as well as imaginative accounts of other happenings.

●   Write the 'Captain's Log of the Starship *Enterprise*' – this might be an altogether more imaginative piece of writing. If undertaken by groups within the class, it could be attempted in the form of a 'cliff-hanger serial': once the story has begun (started by one group or by the teacher) each group should try to extricate the ship's crew from the problem they encounter at the start of their particular 'episode' before moving the story along and leaving the next group with another problem to solve at the end of that section. Hopefully, fans of Flash Gordon, Star Trek and the Star Wars trilogy will be capable of meeting these challenges.

Activity 25: Is there life on Mars?

- Use **Copymaster 5** as a basis for discussion, writing and artwork about whether there really is 'life out there'. Let the children write imaginative stories about the aliens shown on the Copymaster, telling who they are, where they come from, how they live … and of course how we found out about them. This could be written in the form of a descriptive story, or as a conversation between the aliens and Earth people. Perhaps the children would like to invent names for the aliens shown.
- Organise a class debate called 'Let The Alien In?'. Ask the children to imagine that they met up with some aliens whilst exploring space. The debate should focus on whether they would allow the aliens into their spacecraft, with panels of children putting arguments for and against.
- Write imaginative descriptions of UFOs (link this and the above with Art activities). Hundreds of thousands of people have reported seeing unidentified flying objects in the Earth's atmosphere during the past 40 years. Some of these have been explained as stars, weather effects, optical illusions or even as speeding aircraft, but many other reports still seem to defy a rational explanation. Perhaps the children could research some of these cases and present their conclusions.

Activity 26: Signs of the zodiac

- Use **Copymaster 6** to explore and explain the connection between our so-called 'star signs' and the stars in the sky. The Copymaster shows the 12 signs of the zodiac based on 'constellations' or shapes of groups of stars. Let the children identify their own star sign and undertake further research on the grouping and patterns of stars. (**Note:** further work relating to zodiac signs is discussed in the Signs topic in this book, Activity 18, p. 88, and is thus not pursued here.)

Background information

The constellations or groups of stars make various shapes in the sky. Latin names have been given to these shapes, as follows:

Aries (the ram)	Libra (the scales)
Taurus (the bull)	Scorpio (the scorpion)
Gemini (the twins)	Sagittarius (the archer)
Cancer (the crab)	Capricorn (the goat)
Leo (the lion)	Aquarius (the water carrier)
Virgo (the virgin)	Pisces (the fish)

In ancient times, the Babylonians worshipped the Sun, Moon, stars and planets as gods and goddesses. They believed that it was possible to foretell the future by studying the stars. The children should notice that many of the names given to these constellations belong to animals – hence the name 'zodiac', which comes from an ancient Greek word meaning 'to do with animals'.

The zodiac itself was an imaginary pathway in the sky along which the Sun was thought to travel on its yearly orbit. This pathway was thought to be wide enough to contain the orbits of the planets, moons and constellations. It was divided into 12 equal sections, which were called 'signs'.

A person's star sign came from the name of the constellation that hovered above them on the day they were born. During the year the constellations move around the sky, so that by the time of the next birth date, the Earth has arrived back at the same place in its orbit and the same stars are overhead once again. In all, 88 constellations have been named, including the 12 that make up the zodiac.

- Link the space/zodiac theme with pieces of music and poetry: *The Planets Suite* by Gustav Holst is an obvious choice, as are the ballet music of *Horoscope* by Constant Lambert (the movements include 'Dance for the Followers of Leo', 'Sarabande for the Followers of Virgo', 'Valse for the Followers of Gemini' and 'Invocation to the Moon') and *Gemini Variations* by Benjamin Britten. More popular songs, some of which could inspire creative writing or colourful art and craft work, include Jonathan King's 'Everyone's Gone To The Moon', The Kinks' 'Supersonic Rocket Ship', Neil Diamond's 'Stargazer', 'Northern Lights' by Renaissance, 'Silver Machine' by Hawkwind, the LP track version of 'Calling Occupants of Interplanetary Craft' by the Carpenters, and Chris de Burgh's 'A Spaceman Came Travelling'. Poetry could include 'Looking At Stars' by Phoebe Hasketh, 'Space Travellers' by James Nimmo, 'The Witch's Cat' by Ian Serraillier, 'Silver' by Walter de la Mare, 'Startalk' by Robert Graves and 'The Zodiac' by Eleanor Farjeon.
- Perhaps the class could compose a suite of 12 original stories with the zodiac as its theme, each connected with one of the zodiac signs.
- Read or tell the children as many myths and legends connected with constellations as possible. The tales of Hercules, Pegasus, Sirius, Perseus and Orion the Hunter would give much scope for creative writing and art work.

Activity 27: What is a 'black hole'?

- Write 'horror stories' about disappearing into a 'black hole'. Children could imagine that they are adrift in space, perhaps having snapped a security cord on a space walk, as the giant hole appears …. They will of course need a knowledge of the science of black holes.

Background information

Some scientists believe that a number of the giant stars of space may become 'black holes'. As the star fades at the end of its existence, it squashes inwards with an ever-increasing force of gravity. Anything nearby is sucked into the decreasing star – dust, gas, even light itself. As the star is no longer giving off light, it appears black.

Activity 28: The future of space flight

- Consider the future of space flight and exploration. Mention any space initiatives which are currently taking place. Suggest that the children write imaginative descriptions about spacecraft and missions of the future.
- Have we learned all there is to know about the universe? Has the huge amount of money spent on the

space programmes of various nations been money well spent – or could it have been better spent on Earth? Organise a debate on the subject.

- **Copymaster 7** is a 'spare time-filling' fun activity which can be used to fill in spare moments when other work about stars, space exploration and black holes has been completed. Let them complete the maze, finding the correct route through the galaxy.

ART

Activity 29: Your fortune in the stars
- Make a colourful 'Wheel of Fortune' with a hand that can be spun round to settle on one of the horoscopes or fortunes written by children in the class.
- Make pictures of other astrological phenomena – the gypsy fortune teller with her crystal ball, Tarot cards or reading the tea-leaves.

Activity 30: Galaxy pictures
- Make galaxy pictures, representing the four shapes identified in Science Activities (Activity 7). Take sheets of thin blue card or blue paper and create galactic effects by splattering white or silver paint in appropriate patterns. Alternatively, the basic galaxy shape could be printed with white paint, and silver stars could be painted or cut out and glued on to this background design.

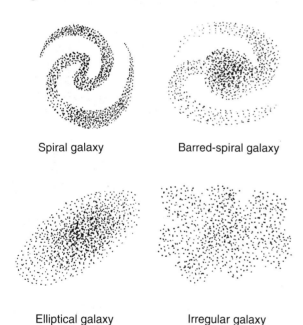

Spiral galaxy   Barred-spiral galaxy

Elliptical galaxy   Irregular galaxy

The four galactic shapes

Activity 31: Life beyond Earth
- Make a large exciting frieze entitled 'Life Beyond Earth'. Incorporate paintings or collages of UFOs, alien craft and, of course, the aliens themselves. Decide whether the background setting for this will be the Earth or an imaginary planet.

Activity 32: Space paintings and models
- Make a star display – every child in the class could contribute a star for the frieze, and write about its formation, existence and eventual demise (link with Science activities). Make stars by painting yellow/gold/bronze outlines, which may or may not be stylised into the traditional star shape, and decorate with gold glitter if this is available.
- Paint 'black hole' pictures. Children will need a large sheet of black paper and white or silver paint (preferably a combination of the two). Lightly brush the swirling outline of the black hole onto the paper. Paint distant 'light' effects, and add silver spray for good effect.

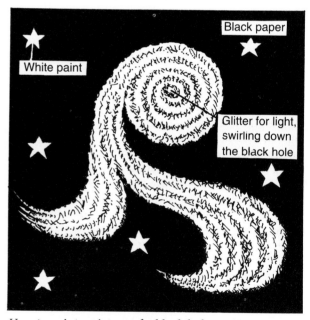

How to paint a picture of a black hole

- Construct a 3-D display of the Solar System. Use balloons as the base for planets: inflate them, cover them with numerous layers of papier mâché and paint them when dry. Alternatively, use various different sizes of ball, related to the comparative sizes of the planets: cover them with Vaseline followed by layers of papier mâché. The vaseline should enable you to release the ball more easily later. When the papier mâché is dry, slice it in half carefully with a razor blade or Stanley knife in order to remove the ball, then seal up the halves again with sticky tape and more layers of papier mâché before painting. (Be aware of safety if the children are handling sharp blades, and ensure close supervision at all times.)

When the 'planets' are completed, add card rings where appropriate. The Sun should be painted or covered with orange paper, with gold and silver rays

144

attached to the sphere. Suspend your Solar System from the classroom ceiling, placing planets in their correct order in relation to the Sun.

● Design and construct model satellites. Remember that they will need imitation solar panels and radio antennae. Let the children decide the function of their satellites, whether for TV or telephone communications, recording weather or observing stars and planets. Perhaps suitable instruments could be designed for them.

● Turn part of your classroom into a corner of space, with appropriate wall friezes of artwork and writing, model astronauts (see Science activities) and satellites suspended from the ceiling.

● Ask the children to paint vivid pictures of 'The Launch', showing the scene of the launch of a space rocket, the clouds of burning, thrusting gas and the rocket heading into a blue sky.

Activity 33: Space age models
● Ask the children to collect as many scrap materials as possible (plastic bottles and bottletops; matchboxes, corks and lollipop sticks; cardboard packets, tubes and cartons of all sizes; nuts and bolts; metal foil; lengths of dowelling; film spools; used light bulbs; cocktail sticks; bicycle reflectors; curtain rings; buttons; pipe cleaners; drinking straws; old pen tops; tin lids; golf tees; cotton reels; scrap balsa wood; wire; old radio valves; plastic tubing; and so on). Use these creatively to make rockets, robots and aliens for your space corner.

Background information
A wide range of suggested craft activities and designs on the theme of space is contained in the book *Space Age Craft* by B.R.H. Targett and M.C. Green, published by Harrap & Co. Ideas include the creation of model rockets, robots, space creatures, missiles and space equipment.

HISTORY ▶

Activity 34: Ideas about our Earth
● Ask the children to suggest how people learned that the Earth is shaped like a sphere. We have not always known this. The ancient Egyptians believed that the Earth was flat and round, shaped like a plate. Investigate Ferdinand Magellan's voyage of exploration in 1520. He sailed right round the Earth, thus proving that it was not flat. Plot the route of Magellan's famous voyage on a globe or map of the world. Relate this to present-day evidence of the shape of our planet as provided by satellites which have circled the Earth and photographed it from every angle.

Activity 35: Pioneers of space exploration
● Find out more about the lives and discoveries of famous scientists who have made significant contributions to our knowledge and understanding of the physical properties of our planet. For example, read about the Polish astronomer Nicholas Copernicus who first suggested that the Earth moves around the Sun. Then find out about the work of Isaac Newton who developed the ideas of Copernicus by establishing that it is the force of gravity which causes the planets to orbit around the Sun, rather than drift away into outer space. The force of gravity is so powerful that it pulls the planets into place, holds the Moon in its orbit around the earth and holds people and objects on the Earth. (Link with Science activities on life in space.) Tell the story of Isaac Newton and the apple tree, whereby Newton is said to have discovered the properties of gravity when an apple fell on his head.

● Investigate the history of space exploration, perhaps focusing on one particular aspect such as the attempts which have been made to land on the Moon.

Galileo

Newton

Copernicus

Pioneers of space exploration

145

Clearly, there is no room here to print full background details of the history of space flight, but the following key facts will provide useful starting points for further research on the topic.

KEY MOON LANDINGS 1959–1972

Sept. 1959   USSR *Luna 2* spacecraft crash lands on the Moon.

Jan 1966   USSR *Luna 9* made the first soft landing on the Moon.

July 1969   USA *Apollo XI* mission – Neil Armstrong is the first man to walk on the Moon.

Nov. 1969   USA *Apollo XII* lands.

Feb. 1971   USA *Apollo XIV* lands.

July 1971   USA *Apollo XV* lands.

April 1972   USA *Apollo XVI* lands.

Dec. 1972   USA *Apollo XVII* lands – on this occasion, two astronauts stayed on the Moon for nearly 75 hours.

Background information

The following extracts are taken from the transcripts of conversations between Neil Armstrong and NASA Headquarters on Earth, on 21 July 1969:

ARMSTRONG: Houston, Tranquillity Base here. The Eagle [code name for the lunar module] has landed …. Going to step off the LEM [lunar module] now. That's one small step for man, one giant leap for mankind … no trouble to walk around … the surface is fine and powdery. I can pick it up loosely with my toe … The dust adheres in fine layers like powdered charcoal to the side of my boots … I only go in a fraction of an inch, but I can see the footprints in the fine sandy particles … It's a very soft surface, but here and there where I plug in the sampler, I run into a very hard surface … [the Moon] has a stark beauty all its own. It's like much of the high desert of the United States …

The astronauts set up various experiments with seismic instruments, a solar wind collector and a laser reflector. They also collected samples of Moon dust and rock which were to be brought back to Earth for scientific analysis.

● Perhaps the children could write what else they think Neil Armstrong might have said during his walk on the Moon. If possible, show the children a film or video recording of this historic event. And what did the astronauts plant on the Moon?

Background information

The US flag was planted on the Moon, and a plaque was unveiled which read 'Here man from the Planet Earth first set foot upon the Moon, July 1969 A.D. We came in peace for all mankind.' It had been signed by the three members of the crew, Armstrong, Aldrin and Michael Collins (orbiting in the command module 'Columbia') together with the President of the United States at that time, Richard M. Nixon. A live TV transmission of the Moon landing was watched by approximately 500 million people on Earth. For UK viewers, Armstrong set foot on the moon at 3.56 a.m., British Summer Time, on 21 July 1969 – truly a historic moment.

● Do the children know what was the first game to be played on the Moon?

Background information

The game was golf – during a subsequent mission, one of the astronauts hit a few practice shots during a Moon walk!

OTHER NOTED SPACE MISSIONS

1957   USSR *Sputnik 1* – first spacecraft to go into orbit around the Earth.

1957   First animal launched into space – USSR's dog Laika. Returned safely.

1961   USSR astronaut Yuri Gagarin became first person to travel in space – in spacecraft *Vostok*.

1962   John Glenn became the first American to orbit the Earth.

1963   USSR astronaut Valentina Tereshkova became the first woman to be launched into space.

1965   USSR astronaut Alexei Leonov became first person to walk in space.

1976   First (unmanned) spacecraft landed on Mars – USA Viking probes.

1977   First spacecraft set off to visit the outer planets of the solar system – USA *Voyager II*.

1989   *Voyager II* flew past Neptune.

● Construct a 'History of Space Flight' wall frieze, with accounts of these and other missions, and illustrations of the spacecraft and people involved.

● Alternatively, construct an illustrated timeline to show key space missions, commencing with details of the launch of *Sputnik 1* (the world's first artificial satellite) in October 1957, an aluminium ball measuring 58 cm in diameter which orbited the Earth for 92 days.

Activity 36: Halley's comet

● Read about Halley's comet and the scientist who gave his name to this phenomenon, Englishman Edmond Halley (1656–1742). Comets are enormous clouds of gas and dust with a core of ice and rock. Edmond Halley calculated from his observations that the comet which now carries his name orbited the Sun and came close to the Earth every 76 years. Try and discover the link between Halley's comet, the Battle of Hastings and the Bayeux tapestry.

Background information

Halley's comet has been seen regularly (every 76 years) over the Earth since 240BC. It appeared in April 1066, shortly before the time of the Norman Conquest, and is therefore shown on a scene in the Bayeux tapestry, a pictorial representation of the events leading up to the Norman invasion of Britain. The Saxons believed that the appearance of the comet was an ill omen, a warning of evil happenings to come. Their worst fears were realised when Harold Godwinsson's army was defeated by that of William of Normandy, in October 1066.

● Halley's Comet was last seen in 1985–86. Let the children calculate when the comet will next be seen. The answer is in the year 2061–62. They can no doubt calculate how old they will be at this time.

If possible, show the children a picture of the section of the Bayeux tapestry depicting Halley's comet.

Halley's Comet, as seen on the Bayeux Tapestry

MATHEMATICS

Activity 37: Space age mathematics

● Make space rocket or robot mathematics work cards:

Ask pupils to perform calculations with the different parts of the robot or rocket, e.g.

head + body − feet = ☐

command module + booster rocket
+ rocket engine = ☐

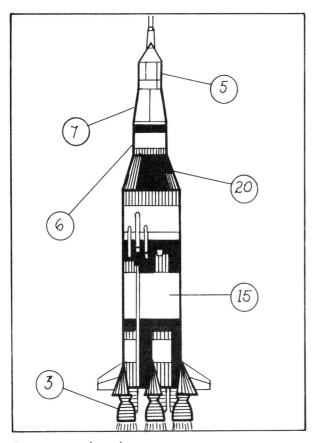

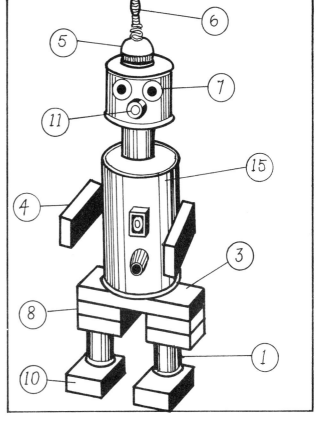

Space age work cards

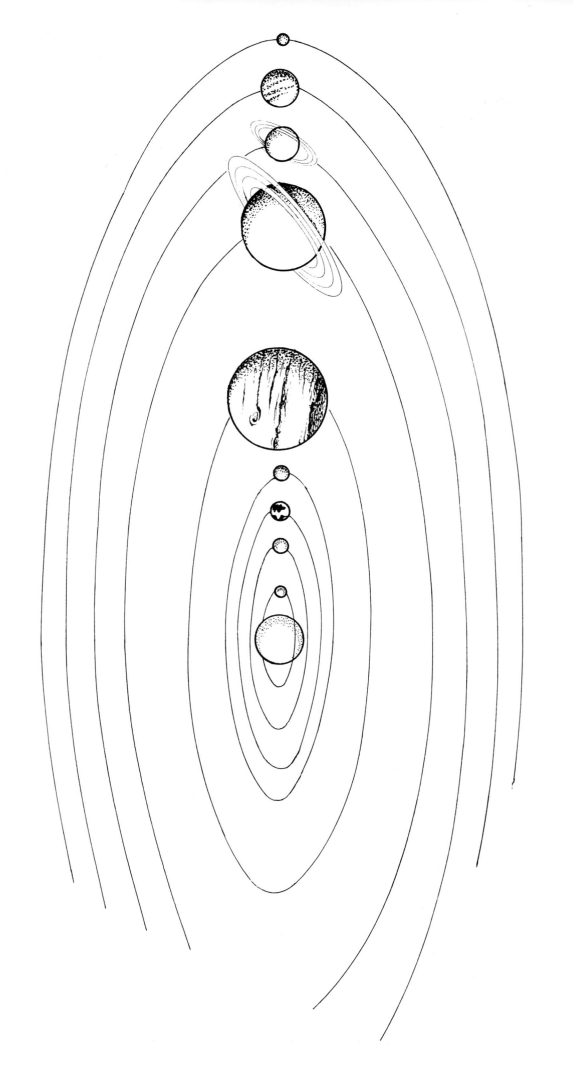

Home galaxy

Origin of the universe: time chart

Event		Millions of years, approximately
Big Bang		0
Galaxies form		1000
Stars develop		4000
Solar System forms		10 000
Life on Earth begins		11 000
Human life begins		14 600
Life today		15 000

Landing on the moon

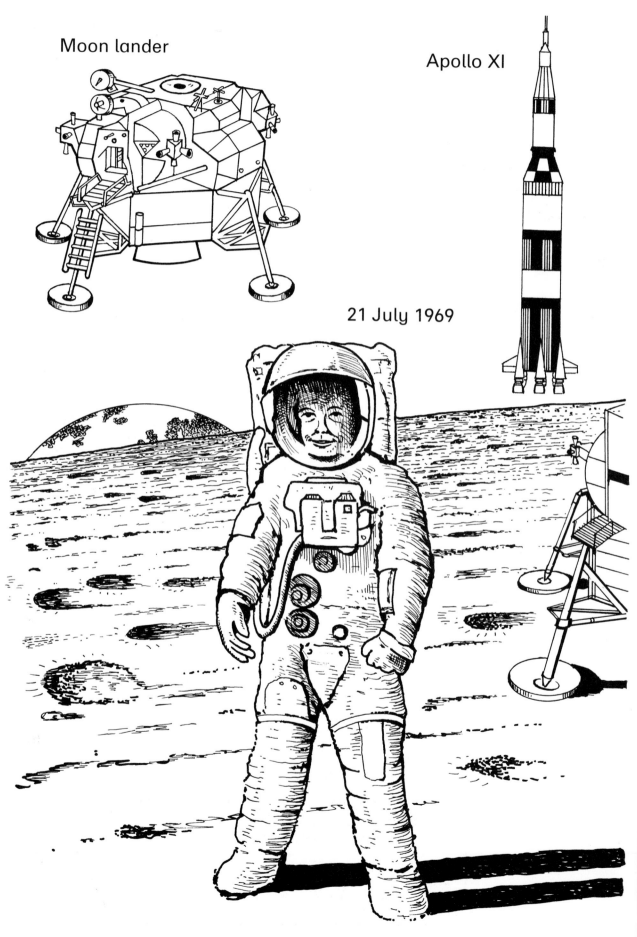

Moon lander

Apollo XI

21 July 1969

Links with space

1

2

3

4

5

6

7

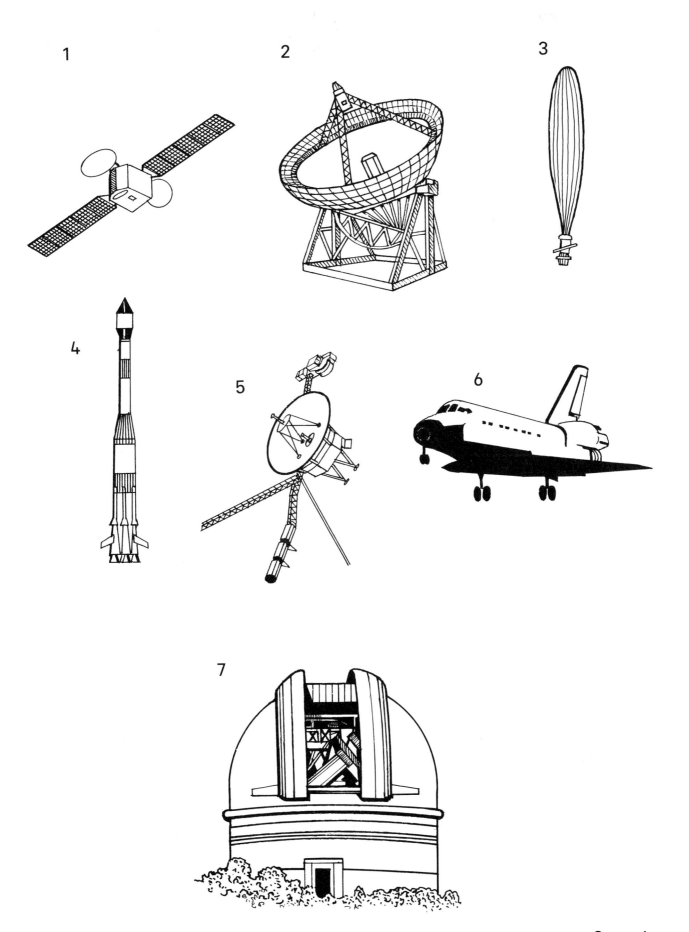

Aliens

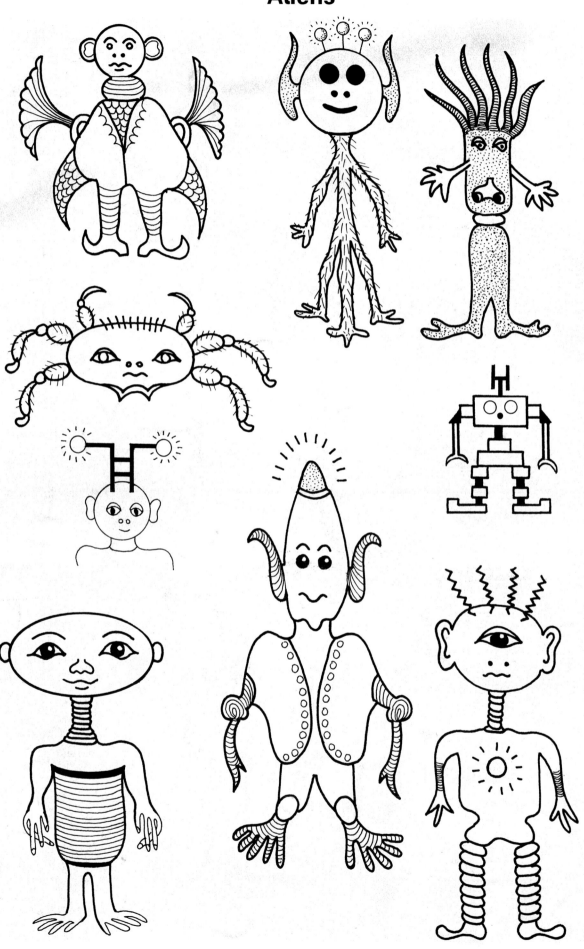

Signs of the zodiac

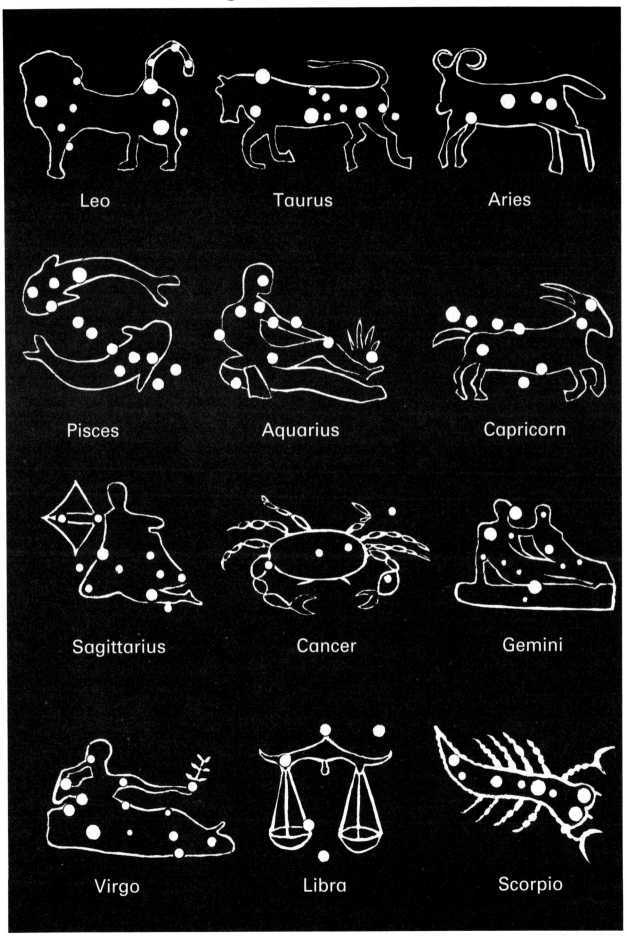

Leo

Taurus

Aries

Pisces

Aquarius

Capricorn

Sagittarius

Cancer

Gemini

Virgo

Libra

Scorpio

Journey to the stars

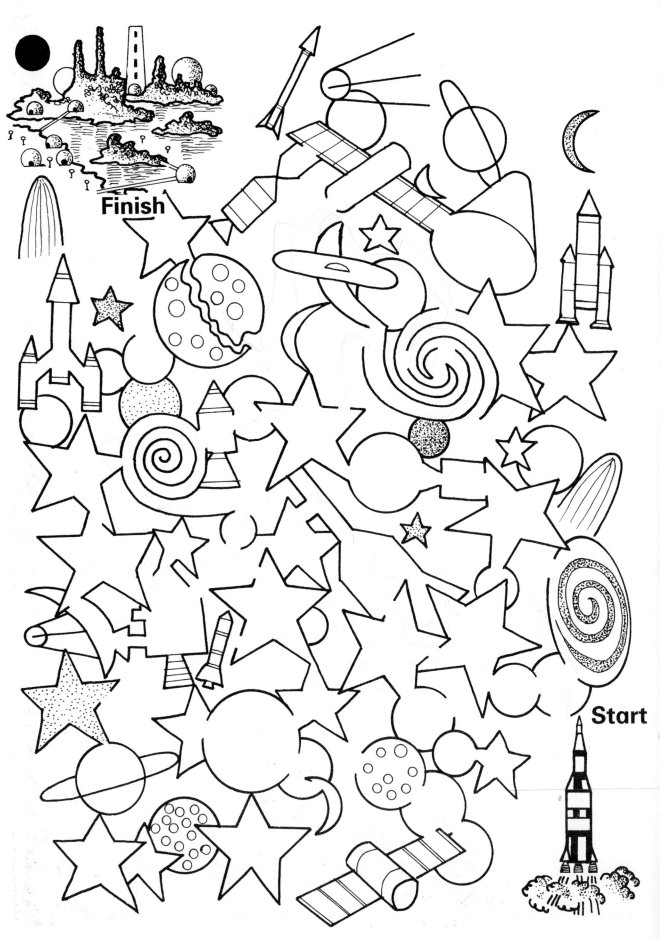

Finish

Start